CARLO SCARPA
THE COMPLETE BUILDINGS

CARLO SCARPA
THE COMPLETE BUILDINGS

TEXTS BY
JALE N. ERZEN

EDITED AND INTERVIEWS BY
EMILIANO BUGATTI

PHOTOGRAPHY BY
CEMAL EMDEN

PRESTEL
MUNICH · LONDON · NEW YORK

CONTENTS

THE COMPLETE BUILDINGS

PREVIOUS. Detail of the concrete wall at the entrance to the chapel at the Brion Tomb, San Vito d'Altivole, Treviso.

INTRODUCTION

Emiliano Bugatti

Carlo Scarpa (1906–1978), one of the most important Italian architects of the twentieth century, worked mainly in Venice and the surrounding Veneto region. He was deeply connected to the local culture in terms of art, architecture and technique. He collaborated with public institutions on permanent and temporary exhibitions and with private clients on houses and tombs. The goal of this publication is to respond to the need to evaluate Scarpa's work within the history of architecture.

Cemal Emden is an architectural photographer who began the photographic mission that led to this book in 2018. To photograph all of Scarpa's works is a demanding and ambitious project. Access to the buildings was one of the most complex aspects, and the organisation of shooting was long and difficult. Many of Scarpa's works do not manifest themselves as icons in public space, exhibiting the strength of mass or structure that we might associate with other modernist practitioners; rather, his buildings often insinuate themselves between existing structures. These are works that give character to and sit in dialogue with places. They also frequently feature a highly detailed design, as if they were art objects rather than architecture. Crucially, these objects are expertly arranged so as never to be isolated; they are always part of a broader framework made up of connections, references, evocations and symbols. In this project, Emden moved within this complexity, entering Scarpa's spaces to explore, discover and ultimately reveal them to the observer.

The book opens with a comprehensive essay by Jale N. Erzen highlighting the complexity of Scarpa, his work, his context and his various influences. The essay rightly reveals connections with the world of figurative art. In doing so, it offers a narrative that goes beyond architectural production to place the architect in a broader sense as a great artist of the twentieth century. Erzen's essay is followed by Emden's photographs, organised chronologically from Scarpa's earliest projects of the 1930s to his final ones in the 1970s. Every project included here has been carefully chosen in accordance with previous publications on Scarpa's output and with the essential support of Luigi Guzzardi, architect, scholar and devoted admirer of Scarpa. Since Scarpa had graduated from the Venice Academy of Fine Arts with a diploma allowing him to teach architectural drawing, but without a professional architecture qualification, he faced opposition from the Chamber of Architects, which refused to recognise him. As a result, Scarpa was not the official architect for some of his projects, and several others were completed by associates. Moreover, after 1978, when Scarpa died, his ongoing projects were finished by collaborators.

Following the photographs are interviews with the owners of two important artisan workshops still active in Venice. This was a wonderful opportunity to include the voices of those who directly witnessed and were involved in Scarpa's working practices, a point of view little explored in monographs. They reveal the materiality of architecture, not only through its material fabric and intricate details but also by shedding light on the process of proceeding slowly through dialogue between the architect and the craftsperson.

This project has been guided by the beauty of and love for Scarpa's works. Certainly, these concepts escape the quantification and limits with which we attempt to rationalise everything around us. Beauty cannot be contained within a theory; it is like love: a disruptive, irrational and at times violent force. Scarpa's works have changed Emden's photography: the complexity of his architecture required new tools and techniques, and this inevitably altered Emden's artistic point of view. His versatile approach to multiperspective photography is a fitting vehicle through which to showcase the sophistication of Scarpa's architecture.

OPPOSITE. Steps in the entrance hall of the Fondazione Querini Stampalia during a day of 'high water' in Venice.

CARLO SCARPA'S WORLD: BEAUTY AND MEANING

Jale N. Erzen

In the almost half a century since Carlo Scarpa's death in 1978, the world of architecture has changed drastically. The 1970s and 1980s were shaken by postmodernist parodies and high-tech style as well as vehement discourse and debate; steel and glass towers began to compete with one another in cities all over the world; and today the skies are filled with the strange architectural gymnastics resulting from the structural evolution of the past decades. Amid all this, Scarpa's relatively small-scale and comparatively quiet works seem to be assured of their longevity, even if, in the haste of the past half-century, quite a few have undergone alterations. Interest in Scarpa is growing; those who visit his works are today awed by the architect's profound attention to detail. There is clearly a growing need for sensitivity, care and beautiful form. One of Scarpa's favourite poets, Paul Valéry, claimed in his dialogue *Eupalinos; or, The Architect* (1923) that 'certain [buildings] are mute; others speak and others, finally – and they are the most rare – sing'.[1] Although for Scarpa architecture was poetry, we can be sure he was aware that his works also had a musical quality.

My first encounter with Scarpa's work dates back more than fifty years, when the architect was still living and creating. Experiencing the Castelvecchio Museum in Verona, restored by Scarpa between 1959 and 1974, left an unforgettable impression that sparked my interest in architecture. In those days, and even in the first decade of the twenty-first century, public interest in Scarpa was scant. The bookshop at the Fondazione Querini Stampalia in Venice, on which Scarpa worked from 1961 to 1963, carried only one book on him, and my friends and I were the only people visiting. On my visit at the time of writing, however, there were more than fifteen books available, and still others had already sold out. There were many visitors, as there were too at the Brion Tomb (1969–78), some 60 kilometres away near Treviso. This renewed interest in Scarpa's work is both astonishing and, at a time when cultural production all over the world can frequently seem to be declining in quality and creativity, perhaps indicative of a growing need for the kind of finesse and sensitivity that Scarpa represents. The spaces he created are other worlds; worlds that do not belong to our hurried, insatiable and often crude existence. In them live a poetic awareness, gentility and care.

There are as many works that Scarpa abandoned, to be finished by others, as there are those that he completed, and among the latter some have been extensively altered; likewise, a few of the posthumously finished works were executed according to the exigencies of the time. We have not included in this book some of the houses on which Scarpa worked because the parts that belonged to him are difficult to separate from the new additions, especially when photographed. The book *Carlo Scarpa: Architecture and Design* (2006), edited by Guido Beltramini and Italo Zannier,[2] has a chapter rich with such fragments by Scarpa, but only those that may be seen as complete have been included here.

This book has been in the making for more than five years, an endeavour that began with the photographic work of Cemal Emden and my modest textual interpretations. In the process, I met many great minds, both in writing and in person. I owe a great deal to the Venetian architect Luigi Guzzardi, with whom every meeting was an intense lesson on Scarpa. Emiliano Bugatti added to my enthusiasm with his excitement and questioning approach. I cannot thank the architect Davide Arra enough for generously accompanying me to Possagno and to the Brion Tomb. His love and enthusiasm for the work was contagious. Of course, it is not possible to adequately thank Cemal, who not only created the foundations of this book with his photographs but enriched it with his superb sense of organisation and his deep insight into architecture.

OPPOSITE. Entrance through the so-called propylaeum of the Brion Tomb in San Vito d'Altivole, Treviso.

Background and Beginnings

The Venetian architect Carlo Scarpa was in many ways an artist unlike any other. His design and architecture work developed in contrast to the atmosphere of a growing and increasingly purist modernism. The architectural scene in Italy witnessed a period of great uncertainty in the postwar period as cities like Rome and Milan saw historic urban memory erased by colossal modern structures. As architects searched for solutions in utopian debates, Scarpa, who was educated in the arts and in design, stood clear of this fervid discourse and experimentation. According to the Italian architectural historian Manfredo Tafuri, 'the highest level of formal coherence was found in the works of those who, seeking refuge from the surrounding commotion, isolated themselves … Historiographical treatment must be suspended in the case of such golden, isolated individuals, and give way to "classical" monographs.'[3] Following Tafuri, we must look at the work of Scarpa as standing clear of any epoch and as belonging instead to all time.

Scarpa began his career in the late 1920s with interior design projects, such as the interiors of the Caffè Lavena in the Piazza San Marco, the Venini glass workshop in Murano and the renovation of the Villa Angelo Velo in Fontaniva, Padua. By the early 1930s he was artistic director at Venini, designing windows and glass works, and in 1935 he embarked on the remodelling of the Great Hall at Venice's Ca' Foscari University, a project that he would return to twenty years later. The knowledge of craft techniques that he developed during his education, such as the creation of different kinds of joint, as well as his experience acquired through glassmaking, gave him insights into the specific qualities of materials, a sensitivity that later became his signature in the intimate details of his architectural designs. His openness to craft, ornament, technique and the boundless possibilities of materials and bricolage distinguishes Scarpa as an artist and designer and is perhaps above all what characterises his modest genius. It was access to the immense possibilities that lie in craft and in the employment of varied materials that opened up for Scarpa the potential of form. Tafuri called him a 'wise artisan' for the design and formal intelligence of his craftsmanship.[4] Scarpa's drawings, rich with minute details and layers of interpretation, attest to this inventiveness.

As Tafuri explains, after 1945, in the aftermath of the Second World War, architecture became an ideology, an instrument of power through which to assert change and to invent solutions to the impasse of modern life. The new architectural avant-garde, which Tafuri describes as a phase of reconstruction, citing such architects as Franco Albini, Bruno Zevi, Ludovico Quaroni, Mario Ridolfi and others, functioned as a deconstruction of fixed history.[5] Between the end of the war and the early 1960s, Scarpa designed several villas, a theatre, works for the Venice Biennale and an apartment building, all seemingly formulated in a secretive language of symbols and interrelated forms, and in a rich array of materials, that could charm and mystify the observer. The exhibition installations that also occupied him throughout these years brought out his extreme sensitivity to artistic content, preparing him for later museum projects. Italy, in trying to revive its artistic heritage, was at the same time drawn to restorations of historical buildings and museum upgrading. Scarpa's contemporary Albini, who worked mostly around Genoa, was also known for working with museums, and Tafuri contrasts him with Scarpa: 'Compared with the quiet murmur of Albini's apodictic signs, Carlo Scarpa's museum projects appear too expressive … On the one hand, then, there was Albini's "let it be" attitude; on the other, there was Scarpa's magisterial narration.'[6] Designing exhibitions for Paul Klee, Piet Mondrian, Antonello da Messina and the drawings of architect Frank Lloyd Wright revealed Scarpa's deep knowledge of the arts and proved him to be as versatile in many facets as the Renaissance masters.

Early commissions such as the Olivetti Showroom (1957–58) and the addition to the Canova Plaster Cast Gallery in Possagno (1955–57) gave Scarpa confidence and a new insight into museum and gallery design. In both projects, Scarpa's understanding of light and the qualities of corporeally experienced space, as well as the interaction between the exhibited works and their environment, makes itself apparent, and this would be the particular language Scarpa would carry into all his subsequent projects, including the Castelvecchio Museum renovation and the Brion Tomb. For Tafuri, Scarpa's complex approach to design, both humorous and at the same time grave and solemnly symbolic, is best exemplified by the Brion Tomb, begun in 1969 and continuing through Scarpa's last years, and the Villa Ottolenghi (1974–78, Bardolino), finished after his death. Although Tafuri emphasises the symbolic qualities of the architect's work, Scarpa's collaborator Sergio Los claims that his works should also be read as elaborate expressions of form: 'In poetic language form is so important that it is difficult if not impossible to distinguish it from the content to which it refers. Seen thus, Scarpa's compositions seem to have no content other than their form.'[7]

For Scarpa, the minutest aspect of any artwork could contain an infinite world of meanings and forms, and this was reflected in his approach to creating. His works welcomed endless articulations, open, like poems, to multiple interpretations and surprises. According to Los, Scarpa's working method involved constant elaboration and then simplification.[8] The drawings that he left of works both executed and aborted bear witness to his immersion in an untiring search for alternatives, for new means of expression. Throughout his life, he stood alone and engaged in continuously perfecting his architectural language, which ultimately became a unique testament to the expression of art's spiritual power through history, as Hegel had claimed.[9]

Scarpa's Venetian Heritage

I am fond of water, perhaps because I am a Venetian.[10]

To gain true insights into the life and world of Carlo Scarpa, one need only watch the footage of the lecture he gave at the Academy of Fine Arts in Vienna on 18 October 1976 – two years before his death – and observe his almost awkward cheerfulness, how happy he was when talking about architecture.[11] As Scarpa comes to the end of his talk, entitled 'Can Architecture Be Poetry?', he is almost dancing. Scarpa was certainly an architectural poet, turning materials and textures into lyricism and rhyme. His work was influenced by Secession architects such as Otto Wagner and the turn-of-the-century spirit brought to the field by the Viennese school, and, of course, by Frank Lloyd Wright. However, when he finally saw Wright's works in person, Scarpa realised how different his own design approach had been. As Los also claims, 'Wright's work had interested Scarpa for years and he had tried to imagine them from publications, but when at the end of the sixties he was able to see it at first hand he was disappointed by the absence of structural details which, he thought, distinguished the new architecture.'[12] Yet the background to Scarpa's creativity as well as his personality, his joyfulness in the immediacy of invention, has to be sought in Venice and the other cities of the Veneto region where he grew up and worked.

The historian Fernand Braudel has drawn upon Le Corbusier's description of Venice as incorporating 'All kinds of techniques, all kinds of materials', so that the city 'teaches us a masterful lesson in harmony'.[13] This poetic description might equally be applied to the multifaceted personality of Scarpa himself. The creation of such a harmony, the way different materials and colours are united, was one of Scarpa's great skills as an artist. We can see this in the second phase of work at Ca' Foscari, in his remodelling of the Great Hall (now Aula Mario Baratto) in 1955–56, where each piece of wood is different in colour, length and the way it is joined. Taken as a whole, the design is an orchestral composition. The figurative in Scarpa's work has the mnemonic background of the Venetian experience: of constantly moving waters, infinite reflections, lights and colours. The harmony of which Le Corbusier writes is an inherent attribute of Venice, seen not only in the way it connects styles, expressions and epochs but in the way each moment that is lived in every corner of the many islands of the lagoon is a richly varied symphony of different hues and atmospheres.

Scarpa characterised himself as 'a man of Byzantium, who came to Venice by way of Greece', a person who looked both inwards and ahead.[14] Venice was a milieu with an important craft tradition, and its many forms of artisanship interested and involved Scarpa. As an artist-craftsman he worked in many techniques, integrating diverse materials such as wood, metal, stone, glass and mosaic, frequently at the same time. The design courses that he received during his art education combined with his Venetian background to create a keen relationship between eye, hand and thought that gave him the ability to combine artistry, craft, construction, calculation and formal excellence. The influences of Venice on Scarpa's art are manifold. One may become aware, for instance, of the relationship between Venice's Byzantine and Baroque sensibility and Scarpa's art by observing the intricate ornaments and luxurious atmospheres, along with the colours and constantly changing light, of the Piazza San Marco. Nevertheless, having distilled these at once joyous and nostalgic moods, Scarpa was a modern Venetian who acted as a bridge between the splendours of the past and the modernism of his time. One need only walk the arcades of the Piazza San Marco with its boutiques, or visit the glittering

Caffè Florian, founded in 1720 and where Scarpa often spent his leisure time, to see how modern he was by contrast. Yet, as his Olivetti Showroom makes evident – itself positioned under the arcades of the piazza – Scarpa also interpreted the finesse and shine of Byzantium in his modern works: glazed brass, crystal glass, laced metal or wooden screens, mouldings and more.

As Tafuri points out, 'There is a risk of abstraction in speaking of Scarpa's relationship with Venice.' But 'his design by "figures," his suspension of "icons of the possible" in dissociated spaces, his use of masking facades, his work on materials and colors all compelling lingering attention, a devoted absorption in the absence of any final syntheses – are strongly reminiscent of Venice as seen through Middle European eyes.'[15] Scarpa, achieving a perfection equal to the finery of historic Venice, strikes a nostalgic tone in reclaiming a past that may no longer be understood. Like the contrasting forms of the late Baroque or the complexity of a Borromini design, Scarpa's work is design taken to its limit, to the exhaustion of all possibilities.

What is Architecture?

As men of our time we have redeemed many things, both morally and socially.
But as architects we have not yet redeemed the form of humble, everyday things.[16]

The great diversity of Scarpa's creative output, ranging from glass, cutlery and picture frames to exhibition design, restoration, original buildings and landscapes, is unusual in the history of architecture. As such, it opens up questions of what architecture is, and who is an architect. Thus it becomes necessary to turn to certain theories and concepts of architecture in order correctly to situate Scarpa within the history of his profession.

As the philosopher Hubert Damisch wrote, the genesis of architecture may be traced to the biblical narrative of Noah's Ark.[17] It symbolises the edifice that protected good people and creatures from the flood, establishing the notion that architecture represents shelter and protection. This idea seems pertinent to those works of Scarpa's that are situated in a city where flooding is common; in the Fondazione Querini Stampalia, for instance, he took the radical decision to invite the waters in: 'Instead of denying entry to it [the water] Scarpa allowed it to flow off more freely, and, by raising the floors in the rooms at risk, guaranteed their continual use. By choosing appropriate materials he reduced water problems to a minimum.'[18] The architect Mario Gemin, responsible for the maintenance of the restoration of the Fondazione, said in a conversation in 2022 that without Scarpa's intervention the floodwaters of November 2019 would have been disastrous for the building.[19] One of Scarpa's last designs, the base of the Monument to the Partisan Woman (1968), a bronze sculpture by Augusto Murer set on irregularly placed stone blocks in the lagoon, may also be interpreted as a symbolic reference to the biblical flood and the protection of the innocents, since the entire sculpture often disappears beneath the rising waters.

The architectural concept of construction is an integral one for Scarpa, whose designs were only fully conceived during the process of their construction and were often not executed according to predetermined plans or calculations. The building up of their form through a gradual assembling of elements evokes the concept of montage, where the whole is composed through the joining of individual parts. Thus, in Scarpa's work, 'construction' signifies the process of building piece by piece over time. For many critics, his drawings attest to the fact that for him, execution and building were the primary principles upon which his design progressed. As the architect George Ranalli notes, Scarpa's method, which consisted in repeatedly layering a drawing so that it acquired depth and intensity, is immediately evocative of the act of construction.[20]

Architecture as body is also an important concept through which to understand Scarpa's architecture. The symbolism of the body was used in many architectural treatises of the Renaissance, notably in churches, which were conceived in cruciform plans, evoking the body of Christ on the cross; with Scarpa, it again came to play a decisive role in relation to architecture: 'the human body, never reduced to a passive measuring system or – worse still – to a "caryatid" of the decorative (symbolic) order, worked as a repository of habits and register of sensations.'[21] Furthermore, the building itself may be conceived as a body, having both an inside and an outside. A representative example in Scarpa's oeuvre is the Villa Veritti (1955–61) as well as the earlier Veritti Tomb in Udine (1952). In both structures, the interior is turned in on itself, introverted, while the exterior is extroverted and looks towards the outside.

In the Veritti house, elements such as the door, the windows and the protruding architectural features are outward-looking. This is also true of the Veritti Tomb, despite its huge circular opening: from the outside, the linear texture of the stone planes helps to keep one's gaze on the exterior wall, and even the circular form of the entrance serves as a symbol of the exterior, keeping the gaze fixed. Once inside, however, one seems to be closed in. One should not understand this to mean that Scarpa's interiors are sealed off and lightless, though. Scarpa often used exterior light as a sculpting and colouring element; light is treated as an ever-changing and conditioning feature that gives the expression of life both to space and to whatever objects it contains.

Architecture has always required an understanding of nature, and Scarpa's works embrace an acute sensitivity to natural materials, seen even in an awareness of the qualities of individual pieces of stone or wood. All his works are adapted to their geography and topology, yet the architect never considered a work finished simply because it had fulfilled its functional requirements and was at home in its environment. It is as though, upon the completion of a work, Scarpa nevertheless always turned back and added a last touch, something extra, even extravagant, like a beauty mark that gives character to a face. For him, no design was ever at an end; a further detail was always called for, such as the drawings and writings he executed on the windows of the Ca' Foscari hall overlooking the Grand Canal.

The Architect-Poet

I have tried to do poetic architecture, but a certain kind of architecture which would emanate a certain sense of poetry for reasons of a formal nature, that is the form expressed could become poetry … Can architecture be poetry? … Of course architecture is poetry. Frank Lloyd Wright said so in a lecture he gave in London. So the answer is: yes, sometimes architecture is poetry, not always poetry. Society doesn't always ask for poetry. Poetry isn't something for every day. You musn't think: I'll produce poetic architecture. You can't say: I'll turn out poetic architecture. Poetry is born of the thing in itself, if the person engaged in it has it in him, this nature.[22]

If one views the world with love and passion, does things with excitement and joy, then this is poetry made not of words but expressed or created in other ways. Scarpa, according to the accounts of his family and friends, was filled with an uncontainable joy when he strolled around the Piazza San Marco, or when he talked about architecture in interviews or lectures. This poetic sensibility was not something casual or easy; he arrived at it through serious thought, hard work and scrutiny, as his drawings, all of which are poetic expressions as well as records, reveal. Scarpa not only created poetry with his architecture or his glass works, which radiate with life and feeling, but he read a great deal of poetry and collected poetry books. When he died, his library contained 241 such books, mostly of French writers including Charles Baudelaire, Stéphane Mallarmé, Paul Valéry, Paul Verlaine and Arthur Rimbaud,[23] as well as many medieval Italian poets, like Dante and Guido Cavalcanti.

The base of the Monument to the Partisan Woman, with its pillars set at irregular heights in the Venetian Lagoon, gathering algae, is a poem written in stone and concrete. That is, Scarpa's base, combined with its placement within the rising and falling waters and the reclining statue that lies upon it, becomes a poetic articulation on the subject of pain and cannot be analysed in any calculable fashion. Not that Scarpa never used calculations; in fact, he conceived his own units of measurement, his own proportional system, which he used to create rhythmic divisions and repetitions. As he explained in a lecture:

I used some tricks. I needed a certain kind of light and I worked out everything on a grid of 5.5 centimeters … In this way you can divide up the parts and you'll never have 150 but 154. Many architects use regulatory plans of the golden section. Mine is a very simple grid which allows for movement – the centimeter is arid, while in my way you obtain a relationship.[24]

This measuring system and the insistent way in which he broke with symmetry and regular order, the way he staggered relationships so that axes break away from their established course, makes Scarpa an anti-Vitruvian, even un-Palladian architect. He insisted that to understand his works one had to remember that he had 'an immense desire to belong inside tradition, but without having capitals and columns, because you just can't do them anymore. Not even a god could design an Attic base nowadays. That's the only decent one … all the rest are junk, even Palladio's in this respect, are just tripe.'[25]

For Scarpa, designing was like writing poetry: he had to be sure of every detail of every element used, as one chooses words for a poem. His designs therefore always took a long time to finish. It is obvious from his drawings that he often changed his mind, conceived new ideas, added details; he could not be forced to work fast. Often, too, he worked on several projects at the same time. This was a way of distancing himself from a work in progress in order to be able to return to it with fresh eyes. The poetic inspiration shows where each element joins the next, as in a poem where each word draws one into a web of references and meanings that can be interpreted from many perspectives. As he installed artworks in a museum space, or even as he placed staircases, balustrades or other architectural features in a building, Scarpa made sure that the empty spaces in between acted as punctuation, giving cadence, breath and measure to the whole. This symbolism also is how Scarpa thought about architecture as poetry, not only because it is poetically aesthetic but because every element and joint can at the same time be metaphoric. Whether visiting Scarpa's buildings, looking at his drawings or tracing his biography, one meets a man who is both an artist – someone who lived with poetry and could at times get lost in his love of art and architecture – and someone who could be practical and humorous. Scarpa, who grew up in the old towns of the Veneto, spent his childhood playing among columns and arches, under Baroque walls and details, surrounded by Byzantine colours and the exuberant variety of the Venetian Gothic. His teaching also reflected his character and his architecture. As Franca Semi, his former student and collaborator, relates, Scarpa frequently used his extensive cultural and literary knowledge when giving his courses, talking often of Valéry, for instance, or of music.[26] Certainly one can conclude that Scarpa's architectural depth and finesse were the fruits of his rich cultural awareness.

Modernity and Tradition

> Modern architecture cannot do without a knowledge of the architectural values that have always existed.[27]

In exploring the complexity of Scarpa's architecture and design, one discovers connections with diverse interlocutors: great architects of the past such as Borromini, or poets and writers like Mallarmé and Proust. The diversity of precedents from which he distilled his personal choices had the effect of creating a modern language as well as constituting in Scarpa a bridge between the past and the present, without following any fashions.

In the way Scarpa created a whole from manifold relationships that are difficult to disentangle, we can see similarities with Borromini, for example the plan of his church of San Carlo alle Quattro Fontane (1638–46) in Rome, in which diverse geometries can be discerned.[28] Likewise, in his detailed analyses and keen insight into the human psyche, we may find a relationship with the way Proust intensifies experience; Scarpa's architecture creates bodily, tactile and visual experiences that are bound together in an intricate and multivalent manner. And the highly symbolic use of language in Mallarmé, whose work Scarpa is known to have appreciated, finds its parallel in Scarpa's ingenious approach to building relationships between architectural elements.

Scarpa's creations thus relate both to the past and to the future, akin to a multispatial and multitemporal sphere tied to the life of materials as well as to the way the eyes and hands work together, a capacity that has evolved over the history of humankind. Yet one of the great achievements of his work is the way every historical reference ultimately belongs to or is brought into the present. One outstanding example of this is the patio inside the entrance to the Istituto Universitario di Architettura di Venezia (IUAV), where, in a contemporary usage, he placed the building's original Istrian stone doorway horizontally on the ground to create a basin or pool.

As noted earlier, Scarpa's versatility found expression in a great many areas of creative production. For Scarpa, no detail was trivial and each was handled with the utmost care and invention; he was aware that architecture is experienced in the sensory details. Whether he was working on a grand scale, as in the Brion Tomb or the Teatro Carlo Felice in Genoa (1963–73), a relatively small space like the Olivetti Showroom, a glasswork or a landscape, he articulated every part so that it could be seen and appreciated for its individual qualities. In the Olivetti Showroom, only 21 metres long and 5 metres wide (69 by 16 ft), different directionalities are created by the orientation of diverse objects – the curving form of the bronze sculpture, the concrete pond, the black marble water basin, the tesserae of the floor – creating singular atmospheres that add up to a complex articulation. We might view the work as a kind of paratactic montage that, taken together, results in formal unity and poetic expression. Likewise in Scarpa's houses, such as the exterior of the Villa Veritti, each individual element – an entrance, a staircase or a balcony – is treated so as to stand on its own, yet creating an orchestrated whole. As one moves from one element to the next, a kind of poetic narration is built up that works against fragmentation.

Both in creating his forms and in connecting his materials, Scarpa worked outside the present; indeed he belonged to all time. His skill was in choosing the position and articulation of an object so as to highlight both the historical reference and create an installation that is always also situated in the present. We might look here at the eternally striking placement of the equestrian statue of Cangrande della Scala at the Castelvecchio, jutting out into space at an angle and orienting the viewer. Scarpa's objects, as they stand in relation to the present and to their environment, act as mnemonic devices, each one opening up to an extended web of artistic and temporal references. Every detail is treated as a discrete work in itself, yet in turn it alludes to a further detail, which may yet be different in form and material – and so on, so that we read the relations in succession like musical notes to make up the character of the whole. As the eminent critic Kenneth Frampton noted, 'Throughout Scarpa's work, the joint is treated as a kind of tectonic condensation; as an intersection embodying the whole in the part, irrespective of whether the connection in question is an articulation or a bearing or even an altogether larger linking component such as a stair or a bridge.'[29] His works open up worlds that have to be travelled through from element to element, as in a painting or a poem, the totality and meaning of which can only be grasped by scrutinising each facet individually. The art historian Vincent Scully remarked of Scarpa's repeated references and unique intermingling of modernism and tradition: 'These relationships with the enduring old are especially moving because Scarpa so dearly loved the early, rather heroic phases of modern architecture.'[30]

Scarpa's *Genius Loci*

To practise architecture also means to learn from and understand nature, and Scarpa's works evidence a heightened awareness of and sensitivity to natural materials and their qualities. To situate a work in its environment is also frequently a matter of how it relates to those natural materials that surround it, whether wood, stone or water. As alluded to earlier, Scarpa tended to use several materials together in a single work, relating their different textures and colours through the use of joints, for instance creating sculpted metal pieces to connect woods of varying types. This profusion of colours, textures and forms creates an integrated whole in which one is reminded both of the underlying natural qualities of the materials and of the craft of the artist. The entrance bridge to the Fondazione Querini Stampalia is one example, as is the Commemorative Stele for the second anniversary of the 1974 bombing in Brescia, a sculptural work of stone, wood and metal that astonishes in its simplicity and enigmatic symbolism. At the Monument to the Partisan Woman, Scarpa let the waters of the lagoon ebb and flow against the stones, creating textures and new colours with the algae that they gather over time. In this work, Scarpa resisted all visible and rigid calculation, allowing each piece of marble to reveal its own character and form while relating to the other materials, whether solid or fluent, that surround them.

Over the course of his career, Scarpa undoubtedly developed his personal architectural and design vocabulary. However, even his last works, such as the Brion Tomb, possess clues that lead us back to his early works, so revealing the way in which certain principles of his vocabulary were there from the very beginning. Nevertheless, in their diversity and richness of detail, no two Scarpa works, no two architectural edifices, are alike. Just as the details and forms of each structure or interior vary in form, colour and character, so each work takes its formal principles from the way it relates to the place in which it is situated. One could mention here again the Aula Mario Baratto, which overlooks the Grand Canal and has been designed so as to keep one's gaze directed towards the waters via a maze of wooden constructions working as partitions. The Fondazione Querini Stampalia is another outstanding example of how a restoration can be designed to relate the building to its environment, beginning with the way one enters it from a sculptural bridge over the canal and the way the stepped entrance indicates the rising of the waters of Venice, and seen also in the metal screen that reflects the movement of the waves and the lights of the canal.

The Villa Veritti is special in the way Scarpa has created a relationship to a site that had no typical character, being neither urban nor rural. He designed two interlocked semicircular forms within a long and narrow parcel of land, creating differing spaces around the house. As one moves around the villa one notices that each elevation relates in different ways to the environment. The architect Boris Podrecca, in his commentary on Scarpa's 'Viennese Point of View', claimed: 'this architecture is accomplished within a space very close to the soil, where its sturdy rooting in the reality of use reflects its link with its *topos*.'[31]

Light, Sacred and Profane

> …all round in level lustre rose
> A shine beyond those shining ones, which grew
> As gathering light on the horizon grows[32]

Like Le Corbusier with his characteristic ribbon windows, Scarpa created windows and openings that were unique to him and whose relationship to light constituted new ways of illuminating a space. A well-known example is the Canova plaster gallery, where he opened up the corners of the building to create dual-sided, vertical inverted windows that ensure that the sculptures are always illuminated as the position of the sun changes; at no time of day is one side of the sculptures left in the dark, as they receive light not only from the windows but reflected off the white walls. With such windows, the movement of the light from east to west and from higher to lower levels creates a continually changing light and makes it possible for the exhibited objects to be viewed in unique ways. Scarpa's openings to let in light are often not distributed according to a symmetrical arrangement across the flat surfaces of a structure; rather, he creates openings where light is needed. At times this may result in an asymmetrical arrangement of varying sizes, shapes and spacings, as can be seen on the long facade of the Banca Popolare di Verona (1973–78).

Scarpa's windows are also often layered, with a frame belonging to the wall and an additional inner cladding. In the Olivetti Showroom, the almond-shaped windows on the mezzanine have a latticed cover that softens the light and creates a movement of shadows. In the Castelvecchio, the Gothic windows are also double-framed, the inner windows having wood and glass and the original outer ones attached to the exterior wall. The round first-floor windows on the wall facing the street at the Banca Popolare di Verona are also double-layered. This gives an appearance of a thick wall, a protected surface. In this we can identify a similarity with Louis Kahn's work, especially the recessed windows of his Exeter Library (1972) in New Hampshire.

One of Scarpa's early works, the Venezuela Pavilion (1953–56) for the Venice Biennale, has a striking cubic form with vertical windows on its upper half that extend onto the roof. A search for exactitude in lighting and interior here leads to an exceptionally modern expression. As the art historian Carlo Bertelli, who knew Scarpa from his student days, wrote in his text 'Light and Design', 'Scarpa was fascinated by Leonardo and loved to attribute his own notions to him on occasion. But here is one of Leonardo's maxims that Scarpa would certainly have subscribed to: "A broad source of light, set high up and not too strong, is that which makes the details of bodies look most attractive."'[33] Scarpa's constant involvement with light manifested in various ways as he transformed it into a multitude of effects. It may be used for its colour-giving properties; it may be softened as it filters through different materials, such as the warm, translucent marble of the cubic windows in the Brion chapel or the wooden grilles of the Olivetti shop; it might be reflected off water or walls or be made to enter space from various angles, as in the Canova Plaster Cast Gallery. Indeed, we might say that Scarpa designed with light, using it as an active architectural and atmospheric element.

Drawings, Joints, Ornaments

His early interest in art and passion for drawing furnished Scarpa with a deep understanding of the language of lines. The experience of drawing from the figure during his student years at Venice's Accademia di Belle Arti equipped him with a rich vocabulary of the line, his command of which can be seen both in his glass designs and in his architecture. His glass designs demonstrate an awareness of curves and concavities that can only be rooted in an engaged experience of looking at and drawing the human figure, while his drawings attest to his exactitude at the same time as they stand as works of art full of feeling. In fact, all Scarpa's design elements, whether geometric or symbolic in form, relate back to his humanism, grounded in classical art and architecture.

Scarpa's drawings, which are kept today in important museums and archives, were often used as direct instructions for the execution of his works.[34] They are traces of his thinking and design methods, as well as records of how his designs took form through constant reflection and revision. In the architectural works themselves, the detailed mouldings and dentils that frequently appear, almost like a private formal language, are akin to lines in a drawing and act to emphasise the lines and forms of other elements; the way he installed mosaics into his walls, floors and pavements also attests to this sensitivity with the line.

From Scarpa's drawings it is obvious that he conceived of his designs in multiple spatial orientations, as layered plans with several different elevations, sections and perspectival views; and the complexity of his finished works is testament to the fact that they were envisaged as complex spatialities and never as a mere arrangement of planes. To achieve this complexity, no simple calculation was possible; as a given design evolved, he discovered new relations to create the whole. As Damisch notes, although Wright was a model for Scarpa, their methods of drawing were very different. For Wright, drawings were representations of his finished works, whereas:

> Scarpa's approach was completely dominated by, paradoxically, the problem of *realization*. From this viewpoint, it seems that the Venetian architect's attitude has curious similarity to that of [Paul] Cézanne. Scarpa harbored the same doubts as Cézanne, if we believe what [Maurice] Merleau-Ponty tells us. And it is this doubt, clearly methodological, that gives his work, seemingly so modest, a historical incisiveness that some consider extraordinary. Now this doubt can be grasped best of all by examining the record of his practice as a draftsman. Herein lies the interest surrounding his drawings, and the ... fact that any analysis of Scarpa's work and discussion of it leads logically and necessarily to the question of his drawings. It is as if we are confronted by an inevitable and perhaps insoluble enigma ... [These are] drawings conceived to be read by others and to back up a demonstration of intent.[35]

Drawing thus functioned for Scarpa not only for construction purposes but as a tool for seeing; it was a constant aid, as it is for many artists, for drawings help to make understood the many phases of perception.

The intricate ways in which Scarpa designed joints, mostly realised in metal, are also witness to his keen sense of line and form and how they relate three-dimensionally. As Frampton has noted, in Scarpa:

> everythings turns on the joint to such an extent that ... the joint is the generator rather than the plan not only in respect to the whole but also with regard to alternative solutions lying latent ... these alternatives arise spontaneously from Scarpa's method, his habit of drawing in relief, wherein an initial charcoal sketch on card, one of his famous *cartoni*, becomes progressively elaborated.[36]

As may by now be evident, it is difficult to talk of a Scarpa work all at once, as a singular unit. And it is joints that, like those in the human body, bring together the multitude of elements to create a whole. Scarpa's joints may also refer to the complex techniques of naval knots. There is certainly a relationship between Scarpa's drawings, where different aspects of a building are related to each other through a variety of lines and super-impositions, and his joints, which are modelled differently according to placement and the material they join. Often, these joints may give the appearance of being aesthetic ornaments; this is true of many structural elements of Scarpa's constructions, which may look ornamental but are primarily structural. The way the metal pieces of the joint encircle or connect to each other is similar to how Scarpa drew his often winding lines.

Many of Scarpa's interventions, as they contribute to the construction of space, can be enjoyed as ornament and furnish the whole with a fine finish. As well as the textural differences of stone, specially designed tesserae and mosaics in pavements, walls and painted panels in carefully chosen colours, and the joints, metal frames and even nails and screws in Scarpa's work can be appreciated as ornament. As the historian of Islamic art Oleg Grabar wrote in *The Mediation of Ornament* (1955), '[ornament] … alone among the forms of art is primarily, if not uniquely, endowed with the property of carrying beauty and of providing pleasure'.[37] This claim would have rung true for Scarpa, evidenced by the fact that Byzantine art was one of his inspirations. Living in Venice, the Byzantine influences visible in St Mark's Basilica, with its ornate facade and golden mosaics, enliven the atmosphere of the entire square both during the day and at night. The use of shimmering gold and the bright colours of the marbles reappear in the works of Scarpa in the form of mosaics and glazed surfaces.

Ornament, besides being a quality of Venetian Baroque and Byzantine art, was also adopted by Scarpa from Viennese Secession architecture and painting, and he was especially inspired by the work of the architect-designers Josef Hoffmann and Otto Wagner as well as the ornamental art and interiors of Gustav Klimt. As the Secessionists reformed the notion of applied and decorative arts at the turn of the twentieth century, so the fine crafts of carpentry and cabinetmaking, among others, were turned into an art in the hands of Scarpa and can be found in many details of his architecture and installations. His affinity with the Viennese school and with Hoffmann in particular also contributed to his furniture designs. In a 2012 documentary on Scarpa directed by Gian Luigi Calderone, Scarpa's son Tobia, also an architect, describes his father as someone who could fall in love with a piece of stone.[38]

Scarpa's fascination with Frank Lloyd Wright also in part stems from how the elder architect integrated ornament into his practice, in elements such as stained or leaded glass and wall reliefs with architectural elements. The influences of the Viennese school, Art Nouveau and the later Art Deco movements can be seen in Wright as well as Scarpa, although the former's embrace of the forms of nature and plant life nonetheless differs from the strictly abstracted, geometric approach of Scarpa. It was rather Klee who constituted the more direct influence on Scarpa with his sense of colour and movement, as seen in the floor mosaics of the Olivetti Showroom, among others. Tafuri has elaborated on the similarity of the work of Scarpa to the paintings of Klee.[39]

Exhibition Design

Scarpa was involved in exhibitions from his early years, first with the glass works that he made for Venini as well as the exhibition halls and display windows he created for the firm. In 1937 he became friends with the art dealer Carlo Cardazzo, who had a gallery and introduced Scarpa to the art circle in Venice. With commissions such as designing the presentations of Arturo Martini and Paul Klee at the Venice Biennale in 1942 and 1948, respectively, and the 1956 Mondrian exhibition at the Galleria d'Arte Moderna in Rome, Scarpa established himself as one of the most important exhibition designers of his time. His involvement with the Venice Biennale and his renovation work at Venice's Museo Correr (1952–53, 1957–60) and Gallerie dell'Accademia (1945–59) furnished him with a deep knowledge of art that led to his crowning achievement in the exhibition and restoration work at the Castelvecchio.

As with many of his works, these projects involved Scarpa in the crafting of metal joints and supports, which he designed for hanging and displaying paintings and sculptures. It also brought to the fore the subject of planes and surfaces as well as wall colouring and texture. Scarpa had very clear ideas about what made a good exhibition space and how to use light, both natural and artificial. In an interview with Martin Dominguez, he described the importance of the pavement in giving character to space – 'The paving is one of the key surfaces in defining the geometry of a room … The objects to be displayed have to be arranged accurately on the paving, to avoid any interference with the geometry of the rooms' – as well as expressing the idea that depth is created not by perspective but rather by the placement of artworks and by light.[40] This is obvious in the exhibition spaces at Castelvecchio: on the ground floor, both the grey pavement and the dark stone pedestals on which the large sculptures stand emphasise the modelling of the figures, with the light coming from the windows in contrast to the grey floor. As is especially evident in the upper galleries at Castelvecchio, Scarpa's exhibition spaces are never crowded and each artwork has its own physical breathing room to bring out its individual qualities.

For Scarpa, not every work that was exhibited had to be perfect; the responsibility of the designer in arranging them was to be able to identify the most interesting or beautiful aspects of a given artwork and to arrange its display in such a way as to make that evident. Whatever the artwork on display, Scarpa's exhibitions had the added effect of emphasising the aesthetic qualities of the work, arranging the display so as to draw the observer's awareness to these aspects. According to the architect Roberto Scichilone, Scarpa's work at the Galleria Regionale della Sicilia in Palermo (1953–54) is an example of 'giving depth with different reliefs and different highlight[s], supporting a culture and a personal taste that complement each other ... By showing something else, he hides what he does not like.'[41]

As a hermeneutic approach, Scarpa's architecture possesses the critical capacity of making one understand that the art object is made visible by means of architecture, and vice versa.[42] This is the magic of his museum and gallery interventions, which combine contrasting angles and positions and juxtapose the different qualities of works; in so doing, they also become a figurative critique of many works of contemporary architecture where repetition becomes cumbersome. Scarpa's knowledge of and insight into how to most effectively design an exhibition was also aided by his intimate experience of the artworks themselves: he would often touch and weigh them in his hands or caress the surfaces of sculptures that would be exhibited. Such tactile experiences certainly added to his visual capacity.

Scarpa and Japan

Naturally the artist I most admired and who taught me most was ... Josef Hoffmann. In Hoffmann there is a profound expression of the sense of decoration ... The reason for all this is very simple: essentially I am a Byzantine and Hoffmann, basically, had a somewhat Oriental character – the character of the European who looks towards the Orient.[43]

Scarpa's fascination with Japan must have been related to its traditional aesthetic practice of combining the natural with the artificial and, especially in its modern architecture, the traditional and the contemporary, because in Scarpa's work it is often these dialectical relations that produce the identity of the object. The intimately tactile quality in Scarpa's work also echoes Japanese aesthetics, where, for example, a ceramic cup is usually not absolutely round, and one has to touch it to fully grasp its delicate form. As in Japanese aesthetics, Scarpa's world is woven of contrasts and discrepancies. He joins the hard and the soft, the dark and the light, the sharp and the smooth, and in each execution this bringing together creates a new whole. The entrance to the IUAV architecture school with its sliding doors, cornices and repeated mouldings is a singular work of art in itself, not unlike the relationship between the natural and man-made, the organic and the highly refined, which combine to form a dynamic unity, that may be discerned in the traditional approach to Japanese aesthetics.

Another aspect of Scarpa's design is the richness he was able to imbue in a limited space. In his teaching, he often used the example of small Japanese gardens, each with fountain, water and greenery, to convey his thoughts.[44] Such an observation can indeed make us aware of the fact that most of Scarpa's designs were executed in limited spaces; even the spacious Brion Tomb can be visually contained from one vantage point.

In his book on Scarpa, Sergio Los emphasises how his architecture works as a symbolic system, an architectural language, that functions as a means to understand or produce a lived reality, rather than the object being the intention or endpoint.[45] As Los claims, conceiving of architecture in this way runs contrary to the common assumption that the object is what offers reality or the knowledge thereof. The emphasis on lived reality and its ephemeral and changing quality, particularly with the effects of time, light and movement, is not unlike the ideas embodied in Japanese aesthetics, where, rather than the object itself, its living quality and relationship to the transitory is stressed.[46]

The Japanese postwar architect Arata Isozaki, in his text on Scarpa entitled 'What Was the Last Dream of Carlo Scarpa?', finds a symbolic resemblance between the great haiku poet of the seventeenth century Matsuo Bashō and Scarpa, noting that instead of visiting prominent places like Kyoto or Nara in the southern part of Japan's main island, known for their significant surviving examples of traditional architecture, Scarpa travelled to Sendai, in the north, not known for having remarkable architecture. Sendai was along the same 'narrow road to the deep north' that Bashō had famously taken.

Isozaki noted: 'The resemblance between Scarpa's work and the careful arrangement of the *machiya* [traditional wooden townhouses] of Kyoto derives, in my view, from the precise combination of materials in each … He must have discovered through his travels in the farthest end of the East anonymous architecture quite akin to his own work.'[47]

Scarpa's visit to Sendai – on his second trip to Japan in 1978 – is emblematic of this spiritual affinity, which inspired him to travel in the footsteps of Bashō. His unfortunate death there may also be interpreted symbolically, since, as Isozaki notes, 'For the Japanese, a journey had a special symbolic meaning – a visit to another world.'[48]

Time and Space: Rites of Passage

The experience of any Scarpa work places us in the passage of time, in the past as well as in the future, through historical references and innovation. Sculptural details like joints or coloured glazes, or even entire works, reveal signs of the process of their making, their relationship to time and to those who observe or occupy them; they are like animated souls alive to our gaze. Scarpa, many of whose works are palimpsests – whether in his layering of elements, materials and spaces or in the temporal complexity of his renovation projects – becomes like a magician, imbuing his constructions with new life. Temporality becomes manifest in dynamic ways through the manner in which Scarpa creates relations between details. In the Brion Tomb, we find ourselves in a landscape of memory and expectation: archetypal forms, cave-like spaces, water channels, reflections, inclined walls, openings in the form of interlocking circles, and myriad colours under the great arch or in the use of tesserae on walls, reflecting light, lead one through an odyssey between life and the mysterious beyond. Scarpa's drawings, too, which reflect layered and superimposed ideas executed in various materials, with thin and thick lines on opaque and transparent papers, are like the labyrinthine landscapes that he executed around and within his buildings. As in his drawings, his spaces take us on a journey of surprising turns, winding staircases, corridors and unexpected passages. In the Castelvecchio Museum, Scarpa created several circulation patterns, each of which creates a different relation to time and space. In the great hall on the ground floor, where the sequence of layered halls leads forwards and produces in the visitor a sense of expectation as to where we are being led, we proceed ahead, viewing the installed works on both sides, each one illuminated differently, sometimes against the light, offering a silhouette, or with side lighting to reveal a worn-out texture. In other rooms, we proceed up and around, or down a narrow corridor, with seemingly unrelated sequences creating a dreamlike wandering. We look up and are surprised to discover a medieval equestrian sculpture, or, looking higher, we find our gaze moving along the multiple layers and different materials of the roof. It is obvious that Scarpa wanted his architecture to create an alternative world of poetry and beauty.

The idea of time as a motor of evolution was introduced in the West during the Enlightenment. The concept of history as a chronicle of events was replaced by historicism as an evolutionary series involving linear progression and forward movement. However, it was in the late nineteenth and especially the twentieth century that time came to be understood as a factor driving movement and memory and as an instigator of change. The trauma of the First World War and the upheaval it brought across the globe made visible and visceral the reality of constant change. Scarpa's life, too, evolved in a world in continual movement: although he had a stable family life and lived mostly in the Veneto, he moved cities and residences many times. For a poet and artist to be, life in the first decades of the twentieth century was one of constant mutation and alteration.

In Scarpa's installations, objects function as temporal maps. They are so placed as to reveal their history in contrast or relation to other objects, and our movement in viewing these objects becomes a movement in time. In the garden of the Fondazione Querini Stampalia, the orientation of the objects leads us from one to the other, creating a flow of time, aided by the flow of the water channelling in diverse patterns and ending in a spiralling pool.

This experience of moving in space and time also unfolds multiple vistas and symbolisms, creating manifold layers of meaning and reference; one is reminded of Dante's vision in Canto XXX of the *Paradiso*, where fantastic images unfold as the layers of a vast rose. Scarpa's works, leading us from one experience to the next, from one aesthetic moment to another, offer constant variety in relationship. In many traditional museum designs, space opens up in front of the visitor as they move from one object to the next, inviting them to progress further and creating a perspective with no end. In the Castelvecchio, however, every path leads in a new direction and what is offered to vision is multiperspectival, drawing the eye up, down and beyond. Scarpa's vistas are constantly changing and multiplying.

The architect's use of light, particularly the exposure of his spaces to the sun's rays at different times of the day and in different seasons, also creates a reference to time that is cardinal in his work, as previously mentioned. But Scarpa's creations also relate not only to history but to his uniquely individual sense of time. This personal sense of temporality makes itself felt in all his works, sometimes by the circulation through his buildings and sometimes by the extension of shadows and the reflection of lights. For the Canova plaster gallery, about which he said that he had 'cut out the blue of the sky', we feel a timeless extension to a sky with boundless depth that likewise enters the museum space and in which we can lose ourselves.[49]

One enigmatic example of the way Scarpa's buildings articulate different ideas of time is the Roman door, mentioned earlier, that he set into the ground beyond the entrance gate at IUAV. The classical object, repurposed with a new function and in a different context and orientation, becomes a thing of the present, travelling from beyond to address us as a newcomer. In a lecture given in Madrid in 1978, Scarpa said: 'I'd like some critic to discover in my works certain intentions I've always had. I mean an immense desire to belong inside tradition.'[50] However, it is simultaneously the case that Scarpa's works always appear modern and never without relation to the present. For the architect, remaining within tradition meant having a sense of reality and beauty that the modern age no longer preserved; as he put it: 'Modern architecture, abstractly stereometric, destroys all sensitivity to framework and de-composition. We have created a void around things.'[51] Venice was a society built upon craft traditions; it could not sever its relation to the Gothic and Baroque passion for detail, colour and lustre. Scarpa's heightened sensitivity to detail, to the precision of application, meant searching for methods and knowledge that may no longer have had a use in modern architecture but which would, in his work, act always to create new experiences. Doors that slide mechanically to open, windows positioned within layers of dentils, mosaic pieces placed in recesses so as to be discovered by surprise – such elements give his works a mnemonic aura.[52]

Scarpa's Legacy

Just as we provide for our necessities, so it seems logical to provide for beauty.[53]

Scarpa's works attest to a deep and inclusive educating force that resists the commodifying effects of the modern culture industry; 'The environment educates in a critical fashion,' he said.[54] In this sense, encountering Scarpa today is to experience spaces of refinement and distillation in a world where growth, quantity and excessive show have become blinding.

Many architects and critics wrote in praise of Scarpa, though there were others who questioned whether he was truly an architect. Bruno Zevi, in a text in which he gives many examples of Scarpa's genius, concludes by asking, 'is Scarpa really an architect?' – for him, Scarpa was not an architect but an artist.[55] As Scarpa's contemporary the Italian architect Ignazio Gardella wrote:

Certainly [Scarpa] was an architect in the fullest and indeed the original sense of the term, i.e. a commander, in charge of construction, not merely a subaltern skilled in tactical operations … Everything had to be wrought up to the highest level of style: the work of architecture, but also the architectural drawing, the shape of a door handle or a hinge, the color of a tie … Yet to Scarpa a shadow which would reveal the shape of a molding was just as important as the proportions of a room … I feel that Scarpa's architecture is impossible to imitate … His architecture is too personal an invention, being born anew on each occasion, and unshackled by any programmatic scheme that can be codified … [It is capable] of communicating to those who appreciate his works an extraordinary emotional resonance.[56]

As these quotes from his colleagues demonstrate, Scarpa's attention to detail, to 'furnishings', to the finery of colours and textures, triggered a great deal of controversy as to his position within the field of architecture. Some, like Manfredo Tafuri, accepted him unquestioningly as an outstanding architect, while others, like Rafael Moneo, went so far as to say that he was a 'Venetian painter', referring of course to his love of colour and light, like Titian.[57] The 1980s still put up definite boundaries between professions, which is no longer the case today, when to accept continuities between fields of interest has become the norm. Thus one of the most rewarding aspects of Scarpa's architecture is the way in which the seemingly most insignificant detail of a design can educate one in the love of exploration and experiment. The philosopher Martin Heidegger's concept of art seems appropriate to describe Scarpa's architecture in its historical references and its poetry: 'Art happens as poetry. Poetry is founding in the triple sense of bestowing, grounding and beginning. Art, as founding, is essentially historical.'[58] Scarpa's works place us in contact with the presence of historical time and our engagement with it. Any contact with Scarpa's creations will inevitably not only make one aware of the deep care and love of art that went into them but, with an almost infectious effect, lead one to wish to explore further our relations to our environment and to the essence of life as it exists in beauty.

OVERLEAF. Lower part of the main facade of the Banca Popolare di Verona.

Notes

1 Paul Valéry, 'Four Fragments from *Eupalinos, or The Architect*', trans. William McC. Stewart, in *Paul Valéry: Selected Writings* (New York, 1964), p. 175.

2 Guido Beltramini and Italo Zannier, *Carlo Scarpa: Architecture and Design* (New York, 2006), pp. 290–95.

3 Manfredo Tafuri, *History of Italian Architecture, 1944–1985* (Cambridge, MA, 1989), p. 111.

4 Ibid., p. 112.

5 Ibid., pp. 3–15.

6 Ibid., p. 51.

7 Sergio Los, *Carlo Scarpa* (Cologne, 1994), p. 26.

8 Sergio Los, *Carlo Scarpa: guida all'architettura* (Venice, 1995), p. 16.

9 G.W.F. Hegel, *Aesthetics*, trans. T. M. Knox, vol. II (Oxford, 1998), Part III, ch. 3, pp. 684ff.

10 Carlo Scarpa, 'A Thousand Cypresses', lecture given in Madrid (summer 1978) [probably at the ID Gallery, where he held an exhibition], in *Carlo Scarpa: The Complete Works*, ed. Francesco Dal Co and Giuseppe Mazzariol (New York, 1984), p. 286.

11 Gian Luigi Calderone, dir., *Carlo Scarpa: fuori dal paradiso – testimonianze* (Pentagram Siftung / Le Stanze del Vetro, 2012), DVD.

12 Los, *Carlo Scarpa: guida all'architettura*, p. 89. See also Vincent Scully, 'Between Wright and Louis Kahn', in *Carla Scarpa: The Complete Works*, ed. Dal Co and Mazzariol, p. 267; and Los, *Carlo Scarpa*, pp. 12–13.

13 Le Corbusier cited in Fernand Braudel, 'Venedik' [Venice], in *Akdeniz, İnsanlar ve Miras* [The Mediterranean: People and Heritage], trans. Aykut Derman (Istanbul, 1977), p. 126, translation by the author. Braudel writes: 'In order to support the weight of Venice, it was necessary to recreate this soil, to strengthen it with stones, furthermore, to support it with thousands, millions of tree trunks that were dug into the earth. Venice rises on a forest that is buried in water ... Venice is a miracle, at least a city which amazes people: here time does not flow as it does elsewhere. As though subjected to a sorcery, Venice has stayed outside of time.' Braudel stresses that in Venice one moves by walking, and this has a distinct effect on the way one perceives the environment. Ibid., p. 115.

14 Carlo Scarpa quoted in Kenneth Frampton, 'Carlo Scarpa and the Adoration of the Joint', in *Studies in Tectonic Culture* (Cambridge, MA, 1995), p. 305.

15 Manfredo Tafuri, 'Carlo Scarpa and Italian Architecture', in *Carlo Scarpa: The Complete Works*, ed. Dal Co and Mazzariol, p. 90. Here 'figure' and 'figurative' are used in a broad sense, referring to symbols, organic shapes and varied applications of form that refer to nature.

16 Carlo Scarpa, 'Furnishings', address delivered for the inauguration of the academic year at IUAV, Venice (1964–65), in *Carlo Scarpa: The Complete Works*, ed. Dal Co and Mazzariol, p. 282.

17 Hubert Damisch, *Noah's Ark* (Cambridge, MA, 2016), pp. 1–25.

18 Los, *Carlo Scarpa*, p. 98.

19 Mario Gemin, conversation with the author, April 2022.

20 George Ranalli, 'The Coherence of a Quest', in *Carlo Scarpa: The Complete Works*, ed. Dal Co and Mazzariol, pp. 259–60.

21 Pasquale Lovero, 'Artist's Proofs (Unnumbered)', in *Carlo Scarpa: The Complete Works*, ed. Dal Co and Mazzariol, p. 224.

22 Philippe Duboy, 'Scarpa/Matisse: Crosswords', in *Carlo Scarpa: The Complete Works*, ed. Dal Co and Mazzariol, p. 170.

23 Rafaella Vendramin, 'Carlo Scarpa's Library', in *Carlo Scarpa: The Complete Works*, ed. Dal Co and Mazzariol, p. 307. Dante was exiled from Florence and settled in Ravenna, and was buried in Rimini.

24 Scarpa, 'A Thousand Cypresses', p. 286.

25 Ibid., p. 287.

26 Franca Semi, *A lezione con Carlo Scarpa* (Milan, 2021), pp. 31, 169, 197, 231.

27 Scarpa, 'Furnishings', p. 282.

28 Leo Steinberg, *Borromini's San Carlo alle Quattro Fontane: A Study in Multiple Form and Architectural Symbolism* (New York, 1977), pp. 15–17.

29 Frampton, 'Carlo Scarpa and the Adoration of the Joint', p. 299.

30 Scully, 'Between Wright and Louis Kahn', p. 267.

31 Boris Podrecca, 'A Viennese Point of View', in *Carlo Scarpa: The Complete Works*, ed. Dal Co and Mazzariol, pp. 241–42.

32 Dante, *The Divine Comedy, III: Paradise*, trans. Dorothy L. Sayers and Barbara Reynolds (London, 1962), p. 180.

33 Carlo Bertelli, 'Light and Design', in *Carlo Scarpa: The Complete Works*, ed. Dal Co and Mazzariol, p. 191.

34 Scarpa's drawings are in the collections of family members, the archives of the Castelvecchio Museum and those of the Museo Correr in Venice, the archives of the Museo Civici di Treviso, and many private collections.

35 Hubert Damisch, 'The Drawings of Carlo Scarpa', in *Carlo Scarpa: The Complete Works*, ed. Dal Co and Mazzariol, p. 209.

36 Frampton, 'Carlo Scarpa and the Adoration of the Joint', p. 307.

37 Oleg Grabar quoted in Jed Perl, 'The Clamor of Ornament: Exchange, Power and Joy from the Fifteenth Century to the Present', *New York Review of Books* 69, no. 13 (18 August 2022), p. 18.

38 Calderone, dir., *Carlo Scarpa: fuori dal paradiso*.

39 Tafuri, 'Carlo Scarpa and Italian Architecture', pp. 86, 89.

40 Martin Dominguez, 'Interview with Carlo Scarpa' (Vicenza, May 1978), in *Carlo Scarpa: The Complete Works*, ed. Dal Co and Mazzariol, p. 298.

41 Roberto Scichilone, 'Installation by Carlo Scarpa at Galleria Nazionale della Sicilia in Palazzo Abatellis', *ARKT-Space to Architecture*, https://arkt.space/en/installation-by-carlo-scarpa-at-galleria-nazionale-della-sicilia-in-palazzo-abatellis, 7 November 2021.

42 Los, *Carlo Scarpa: guida all'architettura*, pp. 8–11.

43 Scarpa, 'Furnishings', p. 282.

44 Semi, *A lezione con Carlo Scarpa*, p. 103.

45 Los, *Carlo Scarpa: guida all'architettura*, p. 7.

46 For the particular qualities of Japanese aesthetics, see for example Jale N. Erzen, 'Tadao Ando in the Light of Japanese Aesthetics', *METU Journal of the Faculty of Architecture* 21, nos. 1–2 (2004), pp. 67–80.

47 Arata Isozaki, 'What Was the Last Dream of Carlo Scarpa?', in *Carlo Scarpa: The Complete Works*, ed. Dal Co and Mazzariol, p. 220.

48 Ibid.

49 Carlo Scarpa, 1981, quoted in Beltramini and Zannier, *Carlo Scarpa*, p. 114.

50 Scarpa, 'A Thousand Cypresses', p. 287.

51 Scarpa, 'Furnishings', p. 282.

52 Ludovico Quaroni, 'Scarpa's "Lessons"', in *Carlo Scarpa: The Complete Works*, ed. Dal Co and Mazzariol, pp. 252–55.

53 Scarpa, 'Furnishings', p. 282.

54 Scarpa, 'A Thousand Cypresses', p. 286.

55 Bruno Zevi, 'Beneath or Beyond Architecture', in *Carlo Scarpa: The Complete Works*, ed. Dal Co and Mazzariol, pp. 271–72.

56 Ignazio Gardella, 'The Gamin', in *Carlo Scarpa: The Complete Works*, ed. Dal Co and Mazzariol, pp. 214–15.

57 Rafael Moneo, 'Representation of the Eye', in *Carlo Scarpa: The Complete Works*, ed. Dal Co and Mazzariol, p. 236.

58 Martin Heidegger, 'The Origin of the Work of Art' (1936), in *Philosophies of Art and Beauty: Selected Readings in Aesthetics from Plato to Heidegger*, ed. Albert Hofstadter and Richard Kuhns (Chicago, IL, 1976), p. 699.

THE COMPLETE BUILDINGS

AULA MARIO BARATTO, CA' FOSCARI UNIVERSITY

Venice, Italy, 1935–37; 1955–56

One of Scarpa's earliest restoration projects was the 1935–37 renovation of Ca' Foscari University, in which he opened up the view on to the Grand Canal in numerous places as well as designing new furnishings for the rectory and offices. He also redesigned the Great Hall (Aula Magna) on the second floor – now the Aula Mario Baratto – where he created wooden fittings and a new frame for the Gothic window. Twenty years later, he was invited to make a second intervention, this time to convert the same room into a lecture hall. Scarpa's work here displays a masterly use of wood, which he used to create a complex screen of wood and metal joints that separates the hall from the entrance. The Gothic windows overlooking the Grand Canal are also separated from the room by a second layer of wood and glass framing. As Scarpa explained, 'I was concerned to explore the relations with the outside world through the apertures and internal layout of space. This is why the wooden pillars are juxtaposed to windows.'[1]

The dividing screen was created from wood reclaimed from Scarpa's earlier restoration project; the vertical columns with their expressive layered design terminating in Y-shaped struts support the wooden beams and gratings of the ceiling. The glazed structure has moveable cloth-covered wood panels that can be closed in order to screen off the lecture hall. The simple seating and the elevated stage with chairs and table were also designed by the architect. A year after Scarpa's death in 1978, a fire ravaged the hall, but it was restored in 1983 by Valeriano Pastor (1927–2023) to Scarpa's exact design.

1   Martin Dominguez, 'Interview with Carlo Scarpa' (Vicenza, May 1978), in *Carlo Scarpa: The Complete Works*, ed. Francesco Dal Co and Giuseppe Mazzariol (New York, 1984), p. 269.

AULA MARIO BARATTO, CA' FOSCARI UNIVERSITY

CASA PELIZZARI

Venice, Italy, 1942

In the early 1940s, Scarpa renovated a house in the historical centre of Venice. In 2000, the house and the internal furniture were sold separately, disfiguring the original project. A few episodes remain, but unfortunately the sense of unity in the architectural and interior design has been lost.

CAPOVILLA TOMB

Venice, Italy, 1943–44

This simple tomb for the carpenter Augusto Capovilla, with whom Scarpa worked on numerous projects, stands out in San Michele Cemetery in Venice for its vertical, pure form. Is stands at almost 4 metres (13 ft) high, with one-third of it extending above the wall behind; an urn set within wing-like extensions contrasts against the dark cypresses behind. In the middle of the tomb structure is a relief depicting the Descent from the Cross. A vertical, tapering cone with a central groove creates a line that terminates at the urn at the top. At the base, a planter stands on a circular support. The monument is carved out of white marble, slightly concave and curved at the corners so as to stand away from the brick wall behind.

CARLO SCARPA | THE COMPLETE BUILDINGS

CASA BELLOTTO

Venice, Italy, 1944–46

As with the renovation of the Pelizzari house, the Bellotto house has also undergone transformations that mean we can no longer get a full sense of Scarpa's original project. The building, which was restored and renovated for a Venetian family of textile merchants, included a shop on the ground floor, storage facilities and offices on the first floor, and the residence on the second and third floors.

CARLO SCARPA | THE COMPLETE BUILDINGS

CARLO SCARPA | THE COMPLETE BUILDINGS

GALLERIE DELL'ACCADEMIA

Venice, Italy, 1945–59

The Gallerie dell'Accademia, Venice's most prestigious museum, is home to the city's largest collection of historic Venetian art. Scarpa was approached towards the end of the Second World War by the director of the gallery, Vittorio Moschini, to undertake restoration and renewal of the museum, which had been badly affected by the war. Scarpa started work in 1945 and initially cleared the spaces of their old curtains and dark furniture, working with a limited budget and simple materials to create as many surfaces for display as possible. He modified the windows and doors by adding a second frame to the entrance in wood and glass and using iron on the exterior. The museum contains early Renaissance paintings, altarpieces and other important works by Venetian sculptors and painters, including the Giorgione painting *The Tempest* (c. 1508). Scarpa cleared the walls of textiles and restored the plaster as well as the colours on the walls, and revised the hanging of the paintings according to period and style. To hang some of the paintings he created new free-standing panels in iron and wood and covered them with cloth. Many of Scarpa's interventions have been altered over the years to comply with legal stipulations or make room for new acquisitions.

CASA GIACOMUZZI

Udine, Italy, 1947–50

WITH ANGELO MASIERI

In this project, Scarpa collaborated with the
architect Angelo Masieri (1921–1952), in whose
name the project was carried out. Scarpa's influence
can be seen in the design of the garden and in
the combinations of internal materials. During
restoration in 1985 the house underwent internal
transformations.

BANCA CATTOLICA DEL VENETO

Tarvisio, Udine, Italy, 1947–49

WITH ANGELO MASIERI

Scarpa collaborated on this project with Angelo Masieri. The interior has been altered but the exterior still presents the building's original character, poised between interpretations of the characteristics of the local architecture and influences from Frank Lloyd Wright.

VILLA BORTOLOTTO

Udine, Italy, 1950–52

WITH ANGELO MASIERI

This private residence was designed by Angelo Masieri with Scarpa's collaboration. It features many aspects of the Wrightian architecture that they both loved. Today, unfortunately, the huge plane tree that was used as an organising element for the L-shaped plan of the villa is no longer in place. On the southern side the building is open to the garden with a white-columned loggia, while the northern elevation features a solid facade more closely related to the Scandinavian organic movement promoted by architects such as Alvar Aalto.

CARLO SCARPA | THE COMPLETE BUILDINGS

VILLA BORTOLOTTO

VERITTI TOMB

Udine, Italy, 1952

WITH ANGELO MASIERI

The design of this tomb was first assigned to Angelo Masieri, a former student and collaborator of Scarpa's, by his second cousin the lawyer Luigi Veritti in 1951, but was offered to Scarpa upon Masieri's death in 1952. Although the final work has many typical Scarpian features, how much of the design belongs to which architect is uncertain.[1] The edifice has an overall rectangular form and its interior is partially covered by a circular metal roof, featuring a small opening in the shape of a cross and imprinted with the word 'PAX' (peace). Its walls are made of Botticino marble panels laid in a linear manner; one enters through a typically Scarpian circular opening, the lower half of which features a pivoting metal gate to the left and a semicircular stone container for flowers on the right. Inside, the ground is covered with cobbles while the left-hand wall houses burial niches in pink marble.

1   Guido Beltramini and Italo Zannier, eds, *Carlo Scarpa: Architecture and Design* (New York, 2006), p. 291; Sergio Los, *Carlo Scarpa* (Cologne, 1994), p. 32. Although Beltramini and Zannier are unsure how much of the design belongs to Scarpa, according to Los many of the formal elements indicate Scarpa's East Asian inspiration.

VERITTI TOMB

SCULPTURE GARDEN, VENICE BIENNALE

Venice, Italy, 1951–52

Within the busy atmosphere of the Venice Biennale, the Sculpture Garden offers a resting place outdoors. By 1948 the biennale's Central Pavilion, located in the Giardini (gardens), needed additions and alterations; these were commissioned to Scarpa, who initially renovated the interior and subsequently created this garden. Three huge pillars, hollowed at the top to act as planters, support a canopy with dramatic circular cut-outs to allow air and light to flow in. The paving is made up of concrete slabs, low brick walls can act as seating, while the adjoining shallow pool with copper water spouts creates a soothing sound that adds to the calm atmosphere.

TICKET OFFICE, VENICE BIENNALE

Venice, Italy, 1952

Scarpa's small and delicately designed ticket office at the entrance of the Giardini della Biennale is no longer in use but stands as a reminder of a finer epoch. The cantilevered canopy, elevated over the glass booth beneath, is a metal-framed structure covered in waterproof canvas. It is supported by three iron masts each with strips of wood that taper slightly at either end. The booth itself stands on a semicircular concrete base finished with wood.

CASA AMBROSINI

Venice, Italy, 1952–53

This small Venetian apartment – with an area of
only 57 square metres (600 sq. ft) – was renovated
by Scarpa using built-in furniture and flexible
partitions to create a space that could accommodate
four people. Most of the interior, including the floor,
is faced with wood. Glazed surfaces reflect light
and together with the warmth of the wood create
a generous interior.

CARLO SCARPA | THE COMPLETE BUILDINGS

MUSEO CORRER

Venice, Italy, 1952–53; 1957–60

The Museo Correr, which occupies two floors of a historic building on the Piazza San Marco in Venice, required renewal after the Second World War; indeed, Scarpa became known for his work in renovating and reinstalling several exhibition sites across the city. The museum includes a Picture Gallery of important works of Venetian painting, including by the Renaissance artists Antonello da Messina and Vittore Carpaccio; the artworks were installed using a variety of methods, including metal supports, wooden easels, free-standing panels and wall mounting. Scarpa changed the hanging in the rooms, which lead on to each other. He lined the walls of the Antonello da Messina room with travertine panelling that stands separate from both the floor and the ceiling; he also differentiated the floors so that the spaces appeared specially designed for the artworks exhibited within. Some of Scarpa's arrangements have been altered over the years, yet the basic principles of his approach to installing the paintings may still be admired.

CASA ROMANELLI

Udine, Italy, 1952–55

WITH ANGELO MASIERI, AND BRUNO MORASSUTTI AFTER MASIERI'S DEATH

Situated on a rectangular plot, this two-storey house stands out with its regularly spaced wood-frame windows and whitewashed structural columns extending to the roof, which spreads outwards as a canopy but allows the light to pass through via a grid of square openings. Inside, the floors, doors and some of the walls and ceilings are faced with wood; the furniture was also designed by Scarpa. The design phase was begun by Angelo Masieri, after whose premature death in a car accident Scarpa took over the project. The Casa Romanelli is similar to the Veritti house in that it also has a pond that reaches to the building's edge, here just outside the living room, except instead of having a circular form it is orthogonal, extending the rectangular plan and echoing the roof and first-floor canopies of this highly geometric house.

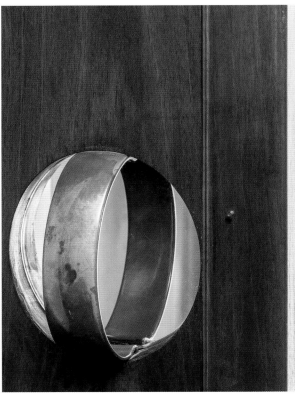

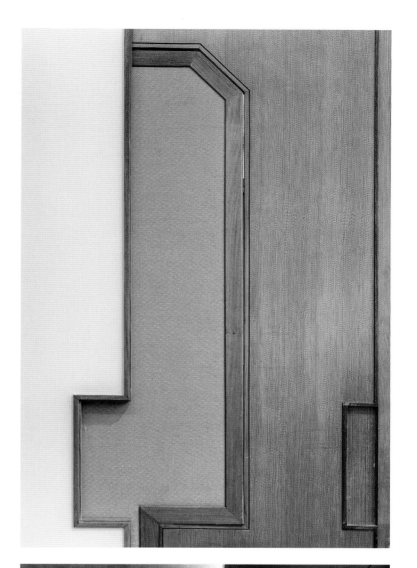

GALLERIA REGIONALE DELLA SICILIA, PALAZZO ABATELLIS

Palermo, Sicily, 1953–54

The commission for the Sicilian gallery of art at the Palazzo Abatellis was given to Scarpa after his work on the 1953 exhibition of works by Antonello da Messina in the Palazzo Zanca in Messina. His sensitive installation won the admiration of the Superintendent of the Galleries of Sicily, Giorgio Vigni, who invited Scarpa to modify the Palazzo Abatellis (which had already been restored following damage suffered during the Second World War) to create a new exhibition space.

The relatively cubic building with Catalan Gothic features, arranged around an internal courtyard, has two floors, and Scarpa installed the sculptural works on the ground floor, including, notably, a bust of Eleanor of Aragon atop a metal plinth with vivid green panelling on the wall behind, lit by direct natural light. The paintings were exhibited on the first floor, mounted to a variety of wooden panels or free-standing supports in wood and metal, sometimes with stucco walls of varying hues.

During the restoration and installation, Scarpa mainly worked in Sicily due to a deadline for the opening in 1954 and the exigencies of the limited budget. This work, with Scarpa's new windows on the restored facade overlooking the courtyard and the subtle design of the courtyard itself, is similar to Scarpa's later restoration and remodelling of the Castelvecchio Museum, while the heavy stone staircase that connects the ground and first floors presages his later exceptional staircase designs, such as that in the Olivetti Showroom.

The art historian Giovanni Carandente, who worked with Scarpa both in Messina and at the Palazzo Abatellis, recalled: 'It is well known that Scarpa was left-handed and could do mirror writing like Leonardo. If ever it should be necessary to renew the plasterwork on the walls of Palazzo Abatellis, whoever scrapes off the 1953 plaster will find numerous phrases and sketches by Scarpa done with the left hand and inverted, like Arabic calligraphy.'[1]

1   Giovanni Carandente, 'Twenty Years of Work', in *Carlo Scarpa: The Complete Works*, ed. Francesco Dal Co and Giuseppe Mazzariol (New York, 1984), p. 204.

CARLO SCARPA | THE COMPLETE BUILDINGS

VENEZUELA PAVILION

Venice, Italy, 1953–56

The Venezuela Pavilion for the 1956 Venice Biennale, located between the Swiss and Russian sites, was Scarpa's first full architectural project. It displays an innovative design with vertical ribbon windows arranged at the upper part of the two spaces, extending over the roof to create abundant lighting. The two rectangular cubes facing each other in a staggered relation with a passage in between can be used as one continuous exhibition hall; the entrance area relating the two spaces has a wooden canopy. The blind exterior walls are of concrete up to the windows, although they were initially intended to be in brick. The inside walls are layered with white marble detached from the floor and ceiling, while the specially arranged exhibition screens are raised on metal frames. In 1968 the original plan was changed, which upset Scarpa's three-part spacing. One of the important features of the pavilion's construction is its extremely light structure in which the concrete roof is carried by two double-sided pilasters. The engineering was done by Carlo Minelli, who was also trained in aeronautic engineering.

The building also has a structure made of metal gratings that was intended as an exit but which is not used today. Despite some renovations in 2016 the building is in need of serious repair, although it is still used for exhibitions. The pavement at the entrance has been raised slightly as a protection against the floodwaters, as has been the case with many Scarpa constructions. A certain formal dialogue may be identified between Scarpa's building and, elsewhere in the Biennale gardens, elements of the Austrian Pavilion with its two rectangular spaces and very simple elevations, designed by Josef Hoffmann in 1934.

VENEZUELA PAVILION   103

GABINETTO DEI DISEGNI E DELLE STAMPE, UFFIZI GALLERY

Florence, Italy, 1956–60

WITH EDOARDO DETTI

After designing the famous Primitivi rooms in the
Uffizi Gallery in collaboration with Ignazio Gardella
(1905–1999) and Giovanni Michelucci (1891–1990)
in 1953–56, Scarpa carried out the restoration of the
Gabinetto dei Disegni e delle Stampe (Department
of Prints and Drawings) alongside Edoardo Detti
(1913–1984). For the exhibition space, now disused,
the pair created metal-framed display cases with
removable glass to allow the replacement of the
drawings on display. The cases are still used today.

BASE FOR THE SCULPTURE
OF THE PARTISAN WOMAN

Venice, Italy, 1955

In 1954 the Institute for the History of the Resistance in the Triveneto commissioned Scarpa to create a plinth for a majolica sculpture by the artist Leoncillo Leonardi (1915–1968). The sculpture, *La Partigiana* (The Partisan Woman, or Resistance Fighter), was unveiled in 1957. However, only four years later it was destroyed in a bomb attack by neo-fascists. Today only Scarpa's support remains, made up of two blocks in concrete – the lower, dynamic form inscribed to commemorate the tenth anniversary of the liberation – connected by means of metal bars. The remnants of Scarpa's base remind one not only of the events of the Second World War and the crucial participation of women in the resistance but also the ongoing struggle against fascism.

COUNCIL CHAMBER, PALAZZO DELLA PROVINCIA DI PARMA

Parma, Italy, 1955–56

This hall is notable for the wooden furniture designed by Scarpa, who designed the tables and seating for Parma's provincial council chamber over the course of a year. The hall is arranged in three parts, with seating for the councillors, seating for an audience and an elevated platform for the council president. The walls are decorated with frescoes by the painter Armando Pizzinato (1910–2004). The entrance, which is separated from the seating by a wooden structure with metal supports, comprises two wooden doors with glazed cubic openings.

COUNCIL CHAMBER, PALAZZO DELLA PROVINCIA DI PARMA

AULA MANLIO CAPITOLO, VENICE COURTHOUSE

Venice, Italy, 1955–57

Scarpa designed this civil courthouse chamber at a time when he himself was a defendant in a case, brought by other Venetian architects who charged that he was practising architecture without a licence. (Scarpa won the case; later, a year before his death, he was also awarded an honorary degree in architecture by the Istituto Universitario di Architettura di Venezia.) Scarpa designed this work gratis and personally assisted in the fabrication of the benches and other furniture as well as the mahogany-panelled walls joined with copper fixings. The small room is given a spacious feeling by the symmetrical three-part arrangement of the magistrates' table and chairs, placed on a platform, the lawyers' tables and the public seating. The wooden door features a metal sculptural mechanism in the form of a scales and a sword, symbolising justice (see p. 339). The room has been kept intact through the careful maintenance of the original craftsmen.

CANOVA PLASTER CAST GALLERY

Possagno, Treviso, Italy, 1955–57

Scarpa's addition to the Gypsotheca (Plaster Cast Gallery) at the Museo Canova in Possagno is noteworthy for its originally shaped corner windows and the iridescent light that emphasises the sculptural forms displayed within. Scarpa was commissioned to create a new wing to house plaster casts and terracotta models by the sculptor Antonio Canova (1757–1822) on the occasion of the two hundredth anniversary of his birth. Responding to the elongated and downward-sloping site, Scarpa designed a long, shallow-stepped hall where the sculptures could be positioned at different levels and on varying pedestals according to their form and size. Some were placed on circular stone plinths, some on horizontal bases, while others were mounted on shelves or displayed in glass cases. The exhibition space is singular in architectural design for the innovative execution of the windows, which are multifaceted and set in the upper corners of the walls, in places projecting into the interior, creating a light that caresses the sculptures from varying angles according to the position of the sun. Scarpa said of his use of light: 'I wanted to cut out the blue of the sky.'[1]

Scarpa's use of white paint on the walls to create a soft light around the white plaster sculptures was an unusual decision in a space where usually a contrast would be sought. As Scarpa explained:

When the moment came for me to decide on the color of the walls, I consulted the officials. So of course, when you have something white, like a plaster cast for example, you would need to use a dark background to make it stand out – it's natural to think in this way. Instead, not because I want to argue with traditional reason, but out of a sort of sudden intuition, I thought it would be better to have a white background because in the other gallery, the larger one, they had chosen ash-gray colors … to make the statues stand out. What sort of color would I have? Black? Impossible, it doesn't reflect at all … I thought white was the best.[2]

In Scarpa's exhibition designs, correspondences between exhibited works and their spaces are created by the relationship of light and the architectural framing. An example is the way the Canova gallery, with its gradually stepped spaces, descends to a luminous fenestration, beyond which is a long pool reflecting its fluid light into the interior. Meanwhile, one side of the hall is largely glazed, while the other is a solid, uninterrupted surface. The play of light between the white of the walls, the white plaster of the sculptures and the pale stone floor creates a constantly vibrating luminosity. Light is treated as an active material and not only as something that affects visuality; it becomes a thing in itself, to be experienced in its diverse colours, reflections, diffusion, sharpness and softness, whether through openings, glazing, reflective surfaces or water.

1   Carlo Scarpa quoted in Sergio Los, *Carlo Scarpa* (Cologne, 1993), p. 58.
2   Carlo Scarpa quoted in Maria Antonietta Crippa, *Carlo Scarpa: Theory, Design, Projects* (Cambridge, MA, 1986), p. 129.

CANOVA PLASTER CAST GALLERY

VILLA VERITTI

Udine, Italy, 1955–61

The Villa Veritti, standing on its narrow plot with
a pool on one side, is a complex arrangement of
architectural elements, each drawing attention
to its singular form. Commissioned by the lawyer
Luigi Veritti, an acquaintance of Scarpa's collaborator
Angelo Masieri, who was designing the Veritti Tomb
(which Scarpa later completed following Masieri's
death), the Veritti house is one of Scarpa's first and
most complete residential designs (it has since
undergone numerous alterations).

The house is located on a rectangular strip of
land in a nondescript residential neighbourhood
in Udine. Scarpa designed a semicircular plan,
with the house having a curved wall on the north
side and tall, wood-framed fenestration joined to
a winter garden open to the south, and a pool as
a half-circle looking west, completing the circle.
Comprising a basement, an elevated ground floor,
a first floor housing the bedrooms and a small attic
with a study, bathroom and solarium, the house
is supported by prefabricated concrete pillars,
between which are placed windows, exposing
the living quarters to the light; inside, the pillars
act as sculptural elements separating walls and
openings. A spiral staircase connects all the floors
and a winding staircase connects the ground floor
with the bedroom level. A balcony on the first
floor extends over the pool, while the entrance on
the east is set beneath a protruding section with
triangular window. The exterior has an extroverted,
expressive quality while the continuously flowing
interior spaces possess a sense of seclusion resulting
from the green-coloured ceiling panel in the dining
room, the warmth of the wooden walls and the
terracotta floor.

CHURCH OF SAN GIOVANNI BATTISTA

Firenzuola, Florence, Italy, 1955–66

WITH EDOARDO DETTI

Although much of the construction of this church was carried out by Scarpa's collaborator on the project, the Florentine architect Edoardo Detti, drawings and plans by Scarpa evidence his decisive work on the design. The southern elevation is outstanding for its plain vertical pillars in stone and its inverted corner windows, similar to those at the Canova gallery. The simplicity and the rectangular volume of this corner structure remind one of certain designs by Louis Kahn (such as the Exeter Academy Library in New Hampshire, USA), whom Scarpa had met in these years. Besides the corner windows, light is filtered through the coloured glass of the front facade as well as through pairs of small square openings on the southern wall of the asymmetrically designed interior. The ceiling is constructed with long wooden planks.

CARLO SCARPA | THE COMPLETE BUILDINGS

CHURCH OF NOSTRA SIGNORA DEL CADORE

Borca di Cadore, Belluno, Italy, 1956–61

WITH EDOARDO GELLNER

This church in Cadore was made to an initial layout by Edoardo Gellner (1909–2004) and was completed in collaboration with Scarpa. The exterior with its walls of linearly textured concrete slabs and steep-sided, copper A-frame roof that gives off a glossy sheen echoes the surrounding forest and Dolomite mountains. Gellner, who had known Scarpa since their student days, was involved in a wider project to build the utopian resort of Eni Village, and in 1956 he approached Scarpa to collaborate on a church design. The concrete trusses of the pyramidal ceiling, braced with criss-crossing metal rods and interfaced with wood, culminate in triangular openings at both ends to introduce light above the altar; light also enters laterally from openings in the lower sides of the hall. It is in the interior of this church especially that Frank Lloyd Wright's influence on Scarpa can be felt.

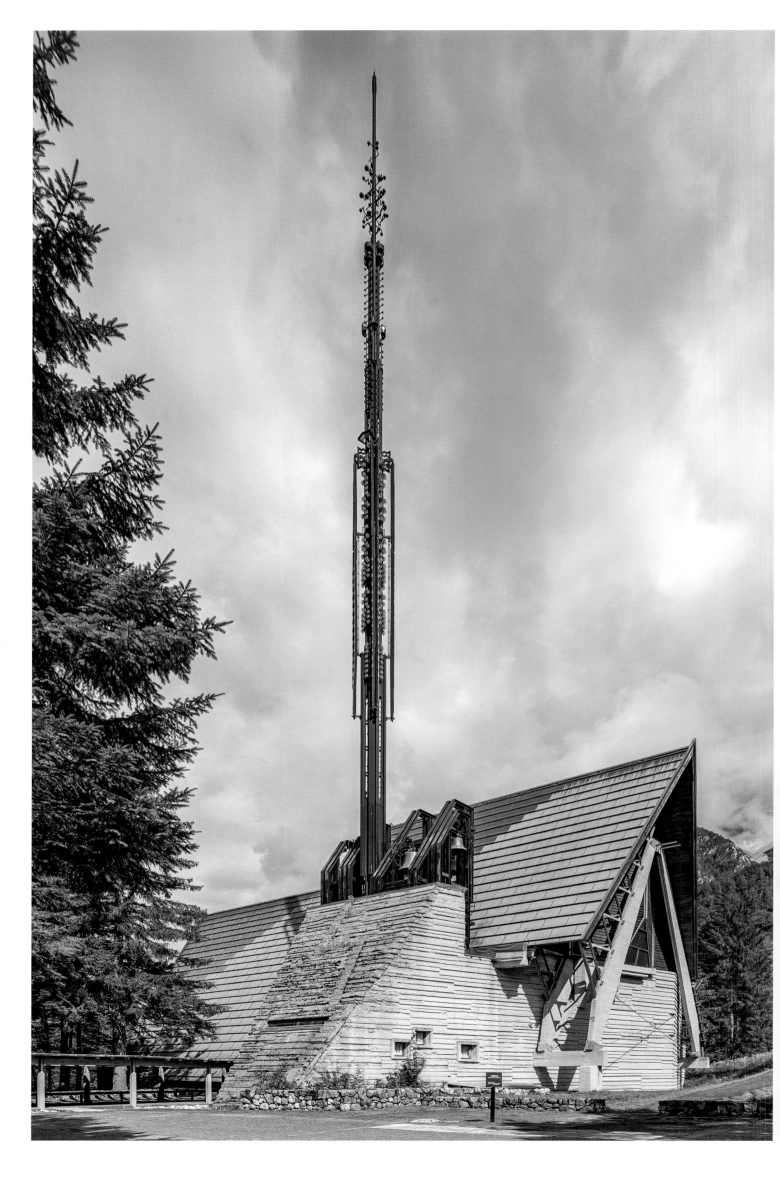

CHURCH OF NOSTRA SIGNORA DEL CADORE

OLIVETTI SHOWROOM

Venice, Italy, 1957–58

On a corner plot among the shops and restaurants of the sixteenth-century arcades on the Piazza San Marco is the Olivetti Showroom, commissioned by Adriano Olivetti after Scarpa won the Olivetti Prize for Architecture in 1956. The showroom is designed both as an invitation to enter and, once inside, to hold one's attention amid the artistically articulated space of the interior. The interior is long and narrow, at 21 metres long and 5 metres wide (69 by 16 ft); Scarpa's achievement is in having manipulated the space to give the impression of an unending installation, carrying the visitor past sculptures, water features, internal windows, mosaic floors, wooden partitions and sliding doors. The space is filled with sculpturally articulated elements, including even the small lavatory within a circular structure.

Though the interior is only 4 metres (13 ft) high, Scarpa ingeniously gave it a spacious impression and sense of dimension by creating mezzanine balconies reached by a shallow, open-sided staircase that provides a visual focus. The floor is composed of a series of differently coloured mosaics in Murano glass. Viewed through the square display window, the space gives a radiant, lustrous impression proper to the classical Baroque atmosphere of its surroundings. The exterior windows are bevelled at 45-degree angles into their metal frames.

In the Olivetti Showroom, walls, window openings, columns and doors all act as individual objects, while bespoke joints and fittings relate the elements to each other. Furthermore, a relation is created between parts through their echoing forms and reciprocal orientation, such as the black marble base that holds the sculpture by Alberto Viani and the graphic form of the stairs that project into the space. The central column, which is original to the building, has been clad in wooden panels and is attached to the mezzanine galleries on both sides with iron bars secured with specially designed joints. The staircase is designed as a cascading form, with the layered steps of varying widths interlocked in a sculptural manner. The almond-shaped latticed windows on the mezzanine have views on to the piazza and the arcade; when closed they soften the light and give the interior a protected feeling, as in many Scarpa designs.

The squared spiral in glazed brass set across four panels of different stones in the wall next to the entrance is lit from behind and is a clue to the way the structural design of the interior can be interpreted as a constellation of relations between spiralling elements, both vertically and horizontally. The intricate metal grating of the front door as well as that on the wall at the back of the ground floor is a recurring Scarpian motif, while many other elements of this important early work would reappear too in later works.

CARLO SCARPA | THE COMPLETE BUILDINGS

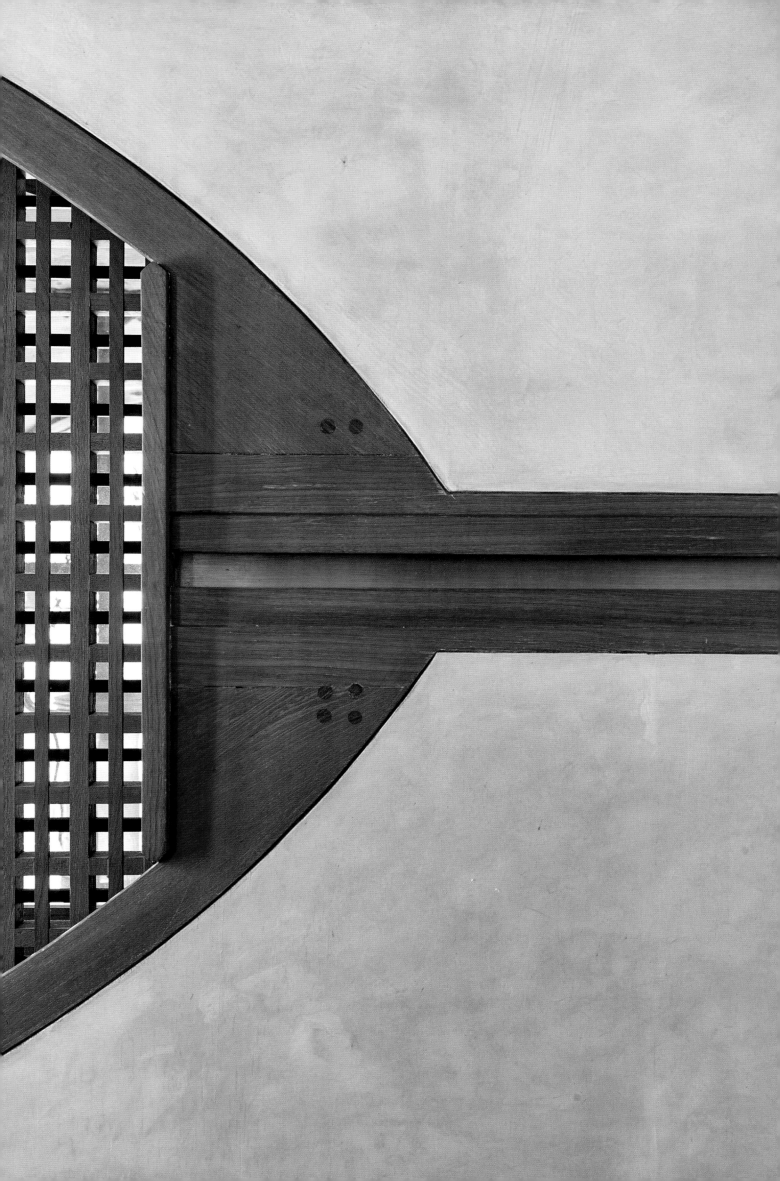

CAMPING FUSINA

Venice, Italy, 1957–59

The structures comprising this lesser-known scheme
by Scarpa – a campsite on the mouth of the Brenta
river, where it reaches the Venetian Lagoon – line
a long main avenue. In sequence, he placed an
entrance pavilion with a circular plan and projecting
winged roof, an extraordinary object to welcome
people; a restaurant-bar; and service blocks with
an unexpected Miesian purism that still preserve
many of their original features.

CARLO SCARPA | THE COMPLETE BUILDINGS

MUSEO DI CASTELVECCHIO

Verona, Italy, 1957–64; 1967–75

In an interview in 1978, Scarpa said of this building: 'The light had to be controlled. I conceived the forms of the windows as a function of the rooms and the exhibits.'[1] The Castelvecchio Museum is one of Scarpa's best-known works; a perfect synthesis of art and architecture as well as of history and the present, it played an important role in the re-evaluation of restoration work as important architectural creations.

The Castelvecchio itself is a castle dating back originally to the fourteenth century; it comprises a compound of red-brick walls around a central courtyard, several towers, a keep and a fortified bridge over the Adige. It was extended during the Napoleonic Wars and was used as a barracks under Austrian rule. Scarpa was commissioned to restore the castle for use as a museum by its director Licisco Magagnato, and worked on it in two phases – from 1957 to 1964 and again in 1967–75 – during which time he set up his studio on the site, producing some 300 drawings, which are today in the collection of the museum.

The almost archaeological work of restoration involved the cleaning and removal of additions and modifications that had accumulated since the Middle Ages, and especially those made in the 1923 during remodelling under its then director Antonio Avena. Scarpa explained of his approach to the heavily modified and historicising building: 'At Castelvecchio everything was fake … I decided to adopt certain vertical values to break up the unnatural symmetry; the Gothic needed it, and Gothic, especially the Venetian Gothic, isn't very symmetrical.'[2] Scarpa also restored the bridge and the exterior brick walls, revealing their historical layering by leaving some traces visible. The simple garden design is enriched with fountains, ponds and low bushes. One of the side entrances to the offices is separated from the garden with a low exterior wall.

In Scarpa's Castelvecchio, the architecture as well as history are on display. It is in this project that he demonstrated the rich possibilities of joints with wood and steel to their fullest degree. Rooms are connected sequentially by arched passages lined with pink stone, and throughout the building Scarpa included various types of staircase and walkways. On the ground floor, medieval stone sculptures are displayed on black stone pedestals, whereas on the first floor, paintings are exhibited at varying angles on easels and metal frames, which also bestow different spatial relations to the works. The labyrinthine circulation around the building finds its apotheosis in the extraordinary positioning of the equestrian statue of the medieval nobleman Cangrande I della Scala. Scarpa positioned the statue at a diagonal angle upon a tall concrete pedestal in an inverted L-shape, hovering over open space at the edge of the courtyard. Its unique and daring positioning is typical of how Scarpa created diverse perspectives in his spaces. He explained: 'The most challenging item was the location of the Cangrande, the equestrian statue. It wasn't easy to work that one out. Even set where it is, up in the air, it's related to movement and conditions it, stressing one of the most important historical connections between the different parts of the castle.'[3]

1   Martin Dominguez, 'Interview with Carlo Scarpa' (Vicenza, May 1978), in Carlo Scarpa: The Complete Works, ed. Francesco Dal Co and Giuseppe Mazzariol (New York, 1984), p. 298.
2   Carlo Scarpa, 'A Thousand Cypresses', lecture given in Madrid (summer 1978), in Carlo Scarpa: The Complete Works, ed. Dal Co and Mazzariol, p. 287.
3   Dominguez, 'Interview', p. 298.

CARLO SCARPA | THE COMPLETE BUILDINGS

COURTYARD, GRAND HOTEL MINERVA

Florence, Italy, 1958–61

WITH EDOARDO DETTI

As with his other projects in Florence, including the Church of San Giovanni Battista in Firenzuola, Scarpa became involved in this project through Edoardo Detti, who was renovating the Grand Hotel Minerva, a historic hotel on the central Piazza Santa Maria Novella. Scarpa was entrusted with the courtyard to the building, which was treated with a brick wall with a highly plastic quality arising from the vibrant movement of the bricks that protrude from the surface and the inserted interlocking diamond-shaped windows.

RINALDO-LAZZARI TOMB

Quero, Belluno, Italy, 1960

The grave designed for Francesca Rinaldo (Scarpa's mother-in-law, after he married Onorina 'Nini' Lazzari in 1934), and later hosting the entire Lazzari family, consists on first sight of a simple horizontal slab. However, it in fact comprises two slabs of Botticino marble raised several inches off the stone support. The frontmost slab is inclined towards the cemetery path and is slightly concave in shape; a narrow central channel bisects the overall form, terminating in a shallow oval basin – demonstrating once again the famous conjoined circles that recur in the master's work. The seam that joins the two slabs and the central channel together form an elegant cross along which the names of the family members are inscribed.

ZILIO TOMB

Udine, Italy, 1960

This burial monument in San Vito cemetery in Udine is different from the others that Scarpa designed over the years. It is a wall tomb composed from six large slabs of Botticino marble with inserts of Istrian stone to form a cross shape; a second cross, formed of slender brass rods, is attached to the top of the vertical panel. The horizontal section features the name of the Zilio family in relief, covered in gold leaf; the lettering, designed by Scarpa himself, is made up of only horizontal and vertical lines and would go on to appear in later projects.

FONDAZIONE QUERINI STAMPALIA

Venice, Italy, 1961–63

The Fondazione Querini Stampalia is of Scarpa's most outstanding renovation projects, including an extraordinary solution to the problem of Venice's *acqua alta*, or 'high water', and was executed by the architect during the same period that he was also working on the Castelvecchio Museum. Scarpa was commissioned by his friend Giuseppe Mazzariol, who was teaching alongside him in the architectural faculty at IUAV and was director of the Fondazione Querini Stampalia, a cultural institution located in a historic palazzo and including a library, museum and archive. The intricate work of restoration involved engineering a solution against the ingress of water and humidity on the ground floor and the vulnerability of the foundations, as well as calculating the exact weights that the ceilings and walls could support.

As in several of Scarpa's restoration projects, the architect had to rediscover and restore the building's original state, in this case seriously distorted and concealed by previous interventions. As the architect Richard Murphy explains: 'Screens of precious and vulnerable plaster are placed over, but detached from the walls, hanging down from the ceiling but terminating above the floor of coarse concrete and at the level of the internal moat where, extraordinarily the flood of waters (the *acqua alta*) are invited by Scarpa into the building.'[1] The great genius of Scarpa was his ability to combine highly technical solutions with artistry. The Fondazione Querini Stampalia shows Scarpa's attention to locality; in contrast to modernist projects that ignored local values, Scarpa here reinterpreted the Venetian spirit in a modern guise.

This work is noteworthy for the progression of its three different areas that are integrated into a continuous whole, ending in an open courtyard. The old palazzo is accessed from an open piazza by an exquisite bridge in wood with finely sculpted railings; descending into the lower gallery space, the visitor encounters a complex series of stepped stones and arched lattice windows overlooking the canal, a design that enables the periodic floodwaters to enter the building itself. One proceeds via a heightened passage to further exhibition spaces and the library, culminating in a courtyard garden. The simplicity of the exhibition hall is contrasted here by more expressive elements, including a lion statue standing over a narrow water channel that terminates in a spiralling font adorned with mosaics.

Scarpa was aided in achieving the complex details of the restoration by a highly skilled technical team including Saverio Anfodillo (joinery), Paolo Zanon (metalwork), Sylvia Fassio (concrete) and Eugenio de Luigi (stucco); he also collaborated again with the engineer Carlo Maschietto, who assisted him on numerous works. Today, maintenance of the restoration is under the responsibility of the architect Mario Gemin.

1 Richard Murphy, *Carlo Scarpa and Castelvecchio Revisited* (London, 2017), p. 33.

Mammalian animals and
Mammiferi e Uomini

GAVINA SHOWROOM

Bologna, Italy, 1962–63

Scarpa's ingenious approach to this rather small space – a commission from the modernist furniture company Gavina – was to accentuate the structural motifs, colouring and texturing them with different materials and light-radiating glazes. From the exterior, the facade of the showroom is formed of a vast concrete slab accentuated with linear channels highlighted in gold leaf; two interlocking circular panes on the left and a single round opening on the right act as windows. The entrance consists of an initial small vestibule followed by a screen door to the interior. As in many small Scarpa interiors, the richly textured and coloured articulation of structural elements such as load-bearing columns, creating a sculptural effect, gives this tight interior a feeling of ample space.

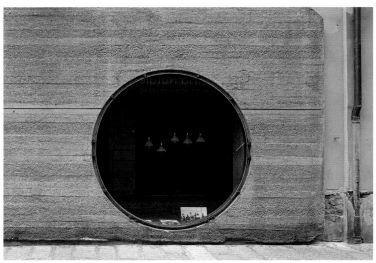

CARLO SCARPA | THE COMPLETE BUILDINGS

CASA SCATTURIN

Venice, Italy, 1962–63

On the top floor of a seventeenth-century Venetian villa, Scarpa created living quarters and a professional office for the lawyer Luigi Scatturin. The two-level space is designed rather like a single piece of furniture in which all the parts interlock to create an indivisible whole. The semicircular walnut table in the office, also designed by Scarpa, is a highlight; the architect named the design 'Signori Prego si Accomodino', or 'Ladies and Gentlemen, Please Make Yourselves Comfortable'. In this large residence, all the partitions, doors, ceilings and wall details are conceived in different colours and materials, from polished coloured stucco to textured concrete to dark wood. Favoured motifs of Scarpa's, such as the use of pearwood, wooden ceilings and the translucent double circle in the corridor, recur here but this time creating a totally new ensemble that constantly changes as one moves through the space. The railings of the balcony on the roof are typically Scarpian. As one moves around the space, one has the impression that colour and silence are the key guides to this work of architecture.

CARLO SCARPA | THE COMPLETE BUILDINGS

MUSEO REVOLTELLA

Trieste, Italy, 1963–78

COMPLETED BY FRANCO VATTOLO AND GIOVANNI PAOLO BARTOLI

In 1963 the mayor of Trieste asked Scarpa to enlarge the Revoltella Museum to incorporate two nearby buildings, including the Palazzo Brunner. The museum is entered through a covered courtyard with nineteenth-century sculptures; the first floor originally had nineteenth-century paintings and the top floor had unroofed rooms for sculptures. The museum was to house a library, conference rooms and offices. The plan had columns attached to the walls to reinforce the old structure and the additions. Scarpa was also asked to increase the height of the building, but he could not complete the project, which he abandoned in 1975. The work was completed in 1991 by Scarpa's collaborators Franco Vattolo (1930–2022) and Giovanni Paolo Bartoli (b. 1936) according to his plans. Thanks to external passages, new exhibition spaces on the roof of the building lead the visitor into a spectacular relationship with the panorama of the city.

FACADE AND TASTING ROOM, FONDAZIONE EDMUND MACH

San Michele all'Adige, Trentino, Italy, 1964–66

WITH SANDRO BOATO AND GIUSEPPE KETMAIER

In 1964, Scarpa began this renovation project at a winery in San Michele all'Adige, housed in an Augustinian monastery dating back to the twelfth century. His relatively small intervention is revealed externally with a concrete base from which the volume of the new entrance in concrete and glass, a bay window and protruding concrete frames stand out as sculptural elements.

ZENTNER HOUSE

Zurich, Switzerland, 1964–68

Designed for Savina Rizzi, the widow of Scarpa's disciple and associate Angelo Masieri, this villa in Zurich is one of the few total works by Scarpa, designed by him down to the last detail, as well as being his only work built outside Italy. The commission involved the transformation of an existing house, and the result evinces Scarpa's love of colour and the myriad qualities of materials. Building regulations did not allow changes to the villa's dimensions or its three-storey height. Most of the changes to the openings were applied on the garden side, while on the other three sides the original openings were kept but Scarpa applied new glass and concrete on the balconies. On these sides, mainly in pink stucco trimmed with brass, one can sense a clear reference to the Viennese school and especially to the master of the *Gesamtkunstwerk*, Josef Hoffmann.

Because of the sloping plot the front of the house is higher, making possible a double-height living room accessed via steps down from the entrance; it is on the same level as the garden on the south side. The bedrooms are on the third floor, again with deep balconies, and the street-facing facade is bisected by a concrete elevator shaft (now covered in ivy) that protrudes beyond the roof. Inside, the floor is in stone; with large windows whenever possible, the interior has a visual continuity with the outdoors. The furniture was also designed by Scarpa: the bar cabinet with thick wooden frames, the dining table in ebony and marble – the precursor to his famous 'Doge' table of 1968 – the sofas, the red fireplace and the wooden doors, some lined with coloured cloth. The wall and ceiling light fixtures on all three storeys are also by Scarpa. The house is seen by critics as having been an open invitation for the architect to demonstrate his creativity in industrial design. Many of the walls and ceilings were painted in ochre or light green with textures varying in tone.

CARLO SCARPA | THE COMPLETE BUILDINGS

CASA BALBONI

Venice, Italy, 1964–74

In the mid-1960s, Scarpa carried out a renovation project in a neo-Renaissance palazzo in the historic fabric of Venice. Scarpa abandoned the project halfway through, but his designs for the connection of the two floors and the relationship to the garden and the canal were kept intact. It was a long and complex process between the project's initiation and its subsequent realisation. Entrance is via a front garden, but the rear facade opens on to the canal; the interior notably allows for a visual permeability between the two ends of the building, obtained by opening the sliding panels that separate the rooms from the central corridor to create a single space. A vertical permeability is also provided by two splendid sinuous openings in the first-floor ceiling, treated with stucco and allowing light to enter from above.

CARLO SCARPA | THE COMPLETE BUILDINGS

ANNEX TO THE CASA DE BENEDETTI-BONAIUTO

Rome, Italy, 1965–72

Scarpa's only project in Rome was this small building built as an annex on a large plot belonging to an eighteenth-century villa. The building has an ovoid plan and its height is bisected by a horizontal ribbon window that opens the interior spaces to the outside. Scarpa wanted to raise the building on walls, leaving the ground beneath free and 'natural'. This aspect has since been modified, with the building now closed at ground level with glazing, but the first floor remains original, where the few rooms are defined through the use of walls with an organic sensibility. The free-standing fireplace emerges as the main internal element, having a central position in the space and with an ovoid shape that echoes the plan.

BASE FOR THE MONUMENT TO THE PARTISAN WOMAN

Venice, Italy, 1968

After the destruction of Leoncillo Leonardi's ceramic *La Partigiana*, leaving behind only part of Scarpa's concrete pedestal, the city of Venice opened a competition for a new memorial sculpture to be situated on a base commissioned from Scarpa. The winner of the competition was Augusto Murer (1922–1985) with his bronze sculpture of a female resistance fighter lying on the ground, her wrists tied and her face displaying her suffering. Scarpa decided to place the sculpture on a platform in the waters of the canal, near the entrance to the Giardini, surrounded by cubic pillars of concrete, faced with stone, in varying heights. The installation was intended to appear or become submerged with the tides. The irregularly placed blocks, together creating an almost chaotic arrangement to evoke pain and confusion, remind one of Peter Eisenman's later Holocaust Memorial in Berlin (2005) with its concrete stelae in different heights.

BASE FOR THE MONUMENT TO THE PARTISAN WOMAN

OFFICES OF LA NUOVA ITALIA

Florence, Italy, 1968–72

WITH EDOARDO DETTI

Carlo Scarpa was invited by Edoardo Detti
to collaborate on this project for the new
offices of the publishing house La Nuova
Italia. From the street, the building appears
as a series of projecting and recessed concrete
volumes punctuated by tall, narrow windows
distributed asymmetrically. A loggia divides
the first floor from the upper ones, with a wall
of glass windows beyond.

MASIERI MEMORIAL

Venice, Italy, 1968–78

COMPLETED BY CARLO MASCHIETTO AND FRANCA SEMI

In the 1950s, Scarpa's frequent collaborator Angelo Masieri commissioned Frank Lloyd Wright to redesign a palazzo on the Grand Canal as a private home. After Masieri's tragic death in 1952, however, his family decided to start a foundation on the same site, in memory of their son, that could be used as a residence and research centre for architecture students. Wright's proposal was rejected by the city planning authority in 1955, and eventually in 1968 Scarpa was commissioned to undertake the project. His design finally gained approval but it was not completed until after his death. He retained the historic fabric of the facade but inside created new, modern spaces for shared use and accommodation. Particularly relevant is the way the new iron beams and concrete slabs match the existing historical walls, touching them only in certain places to create a kind of seam between the old and the new. The concrete floor slabs in the different spaces are laid flush with the metal framework, supported by twin steel columns, to create a geometric ornamental detail while at the same time exposing the structural elements of the building.

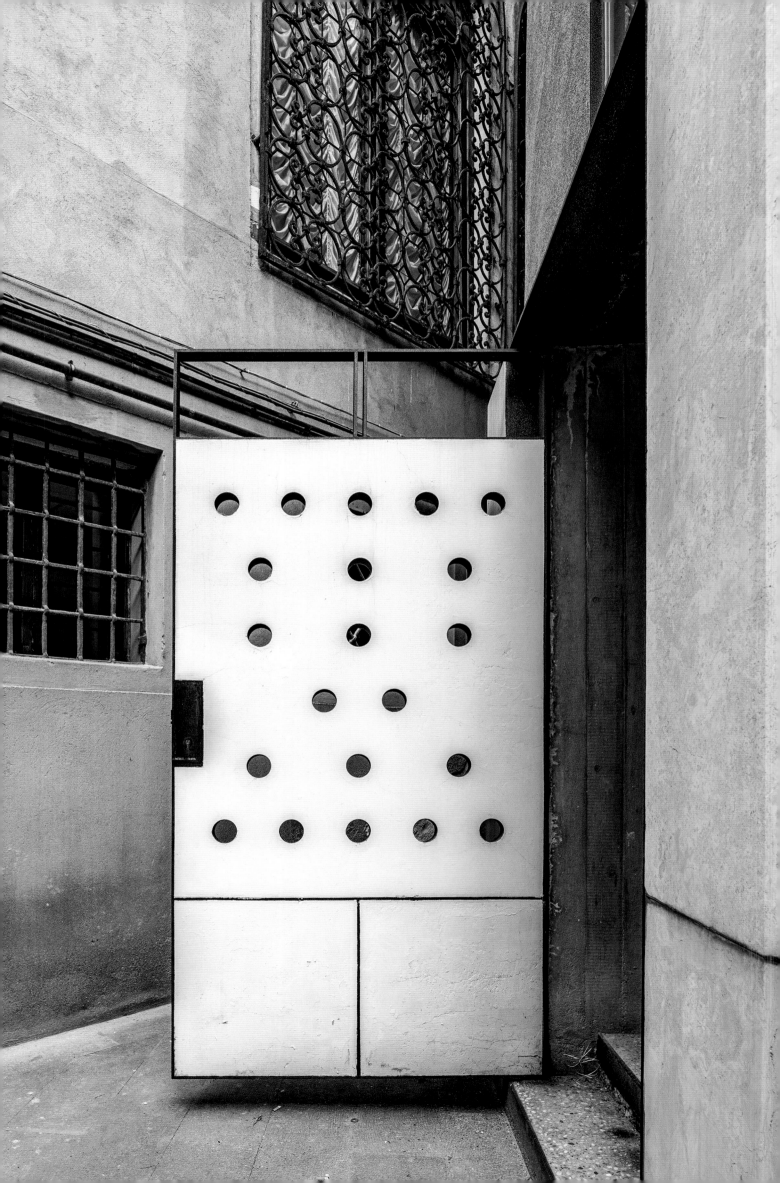

BRION TOMB

San Vito d'Altivole, Treviso, Italy, 1969–78

Scarpa's last major work completed in his lifetime is a composition of complementary forms synthesised into a dynamic whole, in which various architectural elements combine with the symbolic relationships of water. The Brion Tomb complex comprises an L-shaped area of 2,200 square metres (½ acre), adjoining the municipal cemetery in San Vito d'Altivole and purchased by Onorina Tomasin-Brion, the widow of the industrialist Guiseppe Brion. Many critics have found it impossible to define this project, where the architect had full freedom to create a total work of art. It has been called a 'journey' owing to the constant movement it invites visitors to experience.[1] It might also appropriately be called a dream garden, for it features many pools and channels of water; a chapel; an arch (which Scarpa described as an arcosolium, referring to the arched recesses in which early Christian martyrs were entombed) containing the sarcophagi of Giuseppe and Onorina Brion; a meditation pavilion that appears to float on the surface of a reflecting pond; a 'propylaeum', or entrance vestibule, accessed from the main cemetery via an avenue of cypresses; a family tomb covered by a heavy stone roof; and a spiralling cubic form on the water. The exterior wall of the site is inclined inwards to prevent the view from the outside but to also make possible a view from within on to the surrounding countryside. Scarpa had lived in Asolo, near Treviso, and so had a true feeling for the landscape. 'This is the only work I go to look at with pleasure, because I feel I've captured the sense of the countryside,' he said.[2] Scarpa himself was buried here, following his fatal accident in Japan, in a tomb designed by his son Tobia on a plot on the edge of the complex.

This final and monumental work by Scarpa provides many clues to understanding his earlier works. Many of the details, forms and design principles used here can be found in his previous projects, making the Brion cemetery almost a dictionary of Scarpian design. One outstanding feature is the breaking of symmetry and the staggered order in all the arrangements and positionings, somehow hinting at the unexpected and the accidental in life. The propylaeum entrance from the main cemetery, a tall concrete gateway articulated with dog-tooth mouldings, leads one through a darkened space, at the back of which are two interlocked circular openings adorned with blue and pink mosaics – the colours reversed on the other side – symbolising yin and yang. A narrow corridor leads to the meditation pavilion, or 'pavilion on the water', situated on a pond with water lilies. The corridor has a glass and bronze door, built by the Zanon workshop, at the end that can be closed by a mechanical pulley if the waters rise.

The cubic chapel (or *tempietto*, 'small temple') with its bronze-faced altar in one of the corners is

CARLO SCARPA | THE COMPLETE BUILDINGS

richly and subtly illuminated as a result of the differently angled and variously sized openings. On either side are small square windows covered with translucent marble, as well as two vertical windows rising to the ceiling, with layered mouldings; light also enters from above through the pyramidal roof. Made from pearwood and ebony, the roof lets in light from a square opening at the top and is operated by an electrical mechanism. The door leading outside from the back of the chapel is covered with a Japanese *shōji*-style screen, also giving a subtle light. The inner circular door to the chapel, augmenting the Japanese inspiration by evoking the circular windows found in some traditional buildings, is cut off at the base like an omega. The chapel can also be accessed from the rear via a secondary entrance through a cypress garden.

Several recurrent details create continuity among unrelated forms and elements. The faceted, dentil-like mouldings that accentuate corners, sides and edges, sometimes running down to the ground or following a set of steps, constitute a reference to the whole. These mouldings often change in thickness, never becoming repetitious, and in places emerge as surprising elements, such as in the articulation of the pyramidal dome, on the altar and even on the sarcophagi in black and white stone. Another symbolic element proper to a cemetery is the burial chamber, here in the form of the arcosolium beneath which the two sargophagi sit on an area of lowered ground, giving a subterranean feel. Water, in the form of the pools encircling the pavilion and chapel, and the channel of circular basins that descend towards the sarcophagi, is used as a liquid ground from which life emerges. Scarpa's Brion Tomb is a poetic statement about life and death and the inseparability of both, designed to convey a spirit of passion and hope.

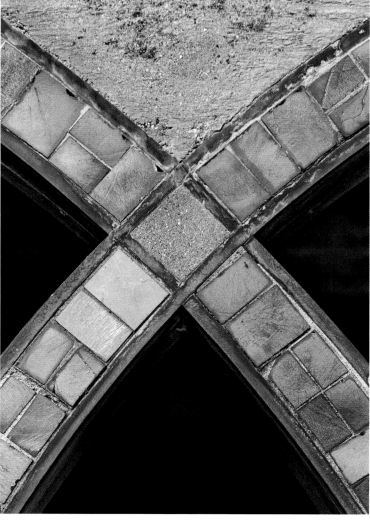

1   Guido Beltramini and Italo Zannier, eds, *Carlo Scarpa: Architecture and Design* (New York, 2007), p. 230.
2   Carlo Scarpa, 'A Thousand Cypresses', lecture given in Madrid (summer 1978), in *Carlo Scarpa: The Complete Works*, ed. Francesco Dal Co and Giuseppe Mazzariol (New York, 1984), p. 286.

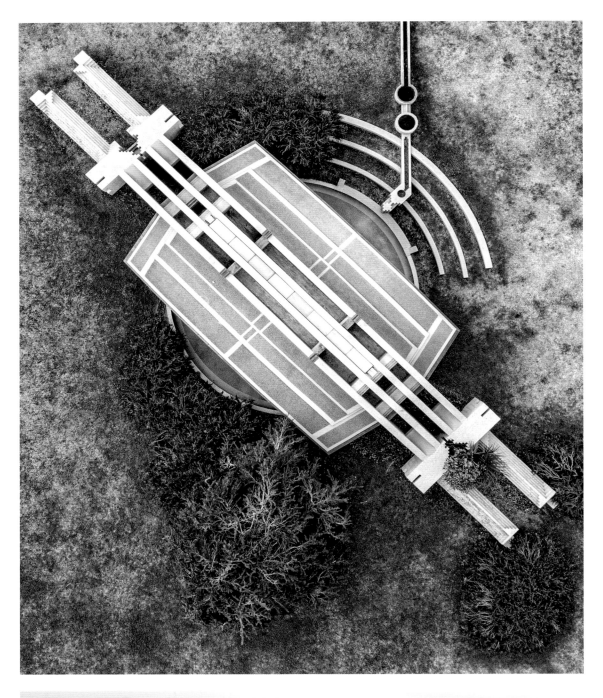

CARLO SCARPA | THE COMPLETE BUILDINGS

BRION TOMB

CARLO SCARPA | THE COMPLETE BUILDINGS

ADDITIONS TO THE VILLA IL PALAZZETTO

Monselice, Padua, Italy, 1971–78

Scarpa's additions and revisions to this farmhouse were first conceived to serve the functions of the farm and the storage and carrying of grain, and to facilitate family living in and around the villa, which dates from the seventeenth century. Scarpa raised the outside pavements and created a staircase to access the villa from the yard on the north, beneath which is a characteristic water pond extending the full length of the house. The courtyard pavement is of special interest: laid in brick with a geometric design of intersecting paths in concrete, it references the farm's original threshing floor. Scarpa added many further aesthetic touches, such as the colourful highlights on the adjacent barn and on the outdoor oven, as well as wooden doors and screens. Metal hinges to operate heavy concrete doors and the graphic, geometric openings in the wall that surrounds the parkland, creating an articulated landscape of passages and vistas, are also among the recurring themes of Scarpa's architecture that are present here.

CARLO SCARPA | THE COMPLETE BUILDINGS

CARLO SCARPA | THE COMPLETE BUILDINGS

LUIGI MARZOLI
WEAPONS MUSEUM

Brescia, Italy, 1971–78

COMPLETED BY FRANCESCO ROVETTA AND ARRIGO RUDI

In 1971 the municipality of Brescia commissioned Scarpa to renovate the fortified keep at the city's castle to create a museum of weaponry. The collection was donated by Luigi Marzoli, an entrepreneur and collector. Outside, two emergency staircases characterise the main facade. The interior spaces are organised with circulation passing fluidly through all the floors, with internal views to enhance the Roman and other archaeological finds and historic items excavated during the restoration. The project was continued and detailed by Francesco Rovetta (1928–2019) and Arrigo Rudi (1927–2007) after 1980.

BANCA POPOLARE DI VERONA

Verona, Italy, 1973–78

COMPLETED BY ARRIGO RUDI

This addition to an old bank building was one of Scarpa's last projects and was finished to his design after his death by Arrigo Rudi, a Verona architect who had worked with him on the Castelvecchio. The facade of the building, which was designed to connect the old structure and the two additions in the middle space cleared by demolition, and which faces the Piazza Nogara, has an almost postmodern expression with its round and square windows in a somewhat staggered distribution; the upper section of the facade is a continuous glass gallery with wooden frames and supported by double steel columns. The cornice above is articulated with Scarpa's typical stepped mouldings, which can also be found lower down on the marble of the facade. The elevation at the back is mostly in glass to allow light into the interior. Inside, walls in polished stucco feature lively colours, and the spaces are organised with special care given to connections and passages.

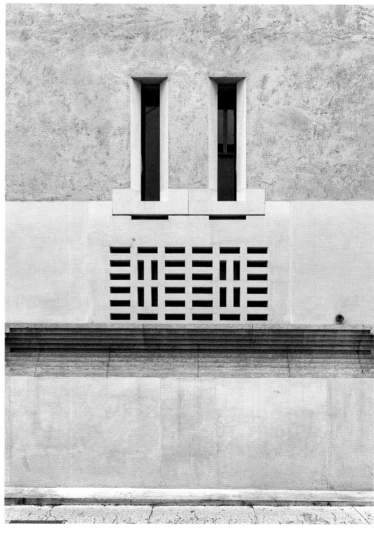

BANCA POPOLARE DI VERONA

COMMEMORATIVE STELE FOR THE SECOND ANNIVERSARY OF THE PIAZZA DELLA LOGGIA BOMBING

Brescia, Italy, 1974–77

This monument commemorates those who were killed or wounded in an attack by far-right militants on anti-fascist protesters in Brescia on 28 May 1974. Though modest in scale, the work took Scarpa a long time to complete, the architect making numerous alterations before arriving at a final design. Facing the Piazza della Loggia, a tall marble column, cubic at the base but becoming cylindrical towards the top, holds an inscribed plaque in the shape of a double cross. In front of the stele, three horizontal wood and brass rods are supported

by two hexagonal bars by way of intricate joints, creating an enigmatic symbolism implying pain. Scarpa's long hesitation in finalising the design had to do with his reluctance to create a work that would contrast with the Renaissance environment; originally, the commemorative column was to be temporary, and Scarpa had intended the whole piazza to contain references to the attack.[1]

1   Guido Beltramini and Italo Zannier, eds, *Carlo Scarpa: Architecture and Design* (New York, 2006), p. 264.

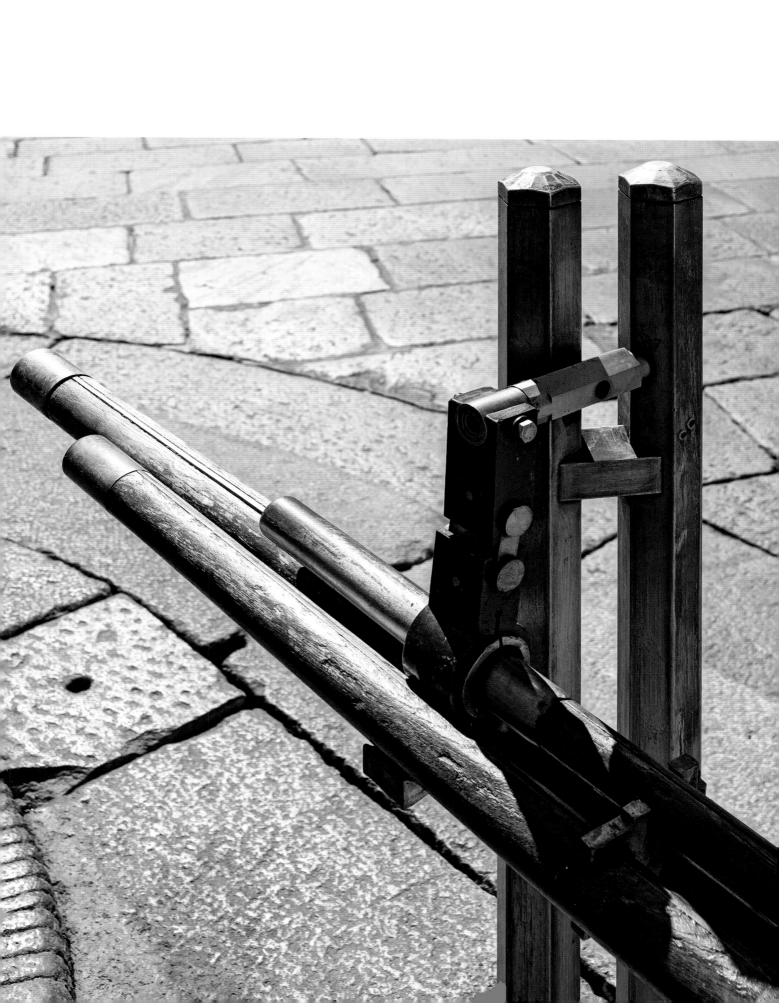

APARTMENT BUILDING

Vicenza, Italy, 1974–78

COMPLETED BY TOBIA SCARPA

This building on the edge of the historic centre of Vicenza is Scarpa's only collective housing project. The building has a curtain wall facing the street, with the facade set back to allow for an open concrete structure that shields the entrance and provides shade, and a perpendicular internal block, forming a T-shaped general layout. The edge of the street-facing facade stands on pilotis, creating a porch that opens on to the common internal garden. The facades feature string courses in reinforced concrete, a white finish that was formerly made of smooth Marmorino stucco, and full-height windows that feature moulded concrete sills and whose placement is offset on each floor. The building is crowned with a parapet with circular windows. The junction between the reinforced concrete pillars and the steel cross-beams, painted bright red, creates distinctive structural 'capitals' around the base of the building.

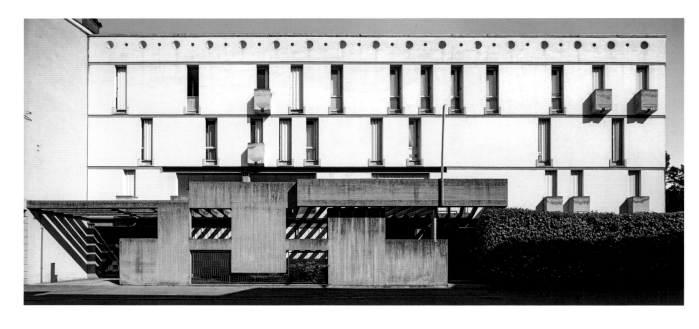

APARTMENT BUILDING 305

VILLA OTTOLENGHI

Bardolino, Verona, Italy, 1974–78

COMPLETED BY GIUSEPPE TOMMASI AND GUIDO PIETROPOLI

The Ottolenghi house, although finished posthumously by Giuseppe Tommasi (1948–2012) and Guido Pietropoli (b. 1945), evidences all the particular stylistic qualities of Scarpa's architecture. For the architectural historian Manfredo Tafuri, the Villa Ottolenghi was one of Scarpa's masterpieces. The house, located on the eastern shore of Lake Garda, is approached through a recessed entrance flanked on two sides by the two wings of the house, which stretch out towards the landscape as if wings in flight. The roof's geometric layout reflects the spatial partitions of the interior, and its paved surface is topped with a ventilation shaft in interlocking cylindrical form, a repeated motif in Scarpa's work. The house is partially sunk into the ground so that the roof joins the surrounding steep landscape and becomes a terrace.

There are interesting correspondences on the exterior of the building, with the pool and projecting chimney bearing similarities in their angular forms. Access is via steps in an asymmetrical facade with various rough and smooth wall surfaces and textured, layered columns. As with many of Scarpa's projects, such structural features have both a functional purpose and an ornamental one. Coloured panels, a variety of materials, the play of light entering the building as well as the sound of water and even wind together create a rich array of sensory effects. Visited in February, the vivid yellow of the mimosa trees against the light grey of the walls adds to the vibrant atmosphere and is a further example of how this man-made structure embraces its environment.

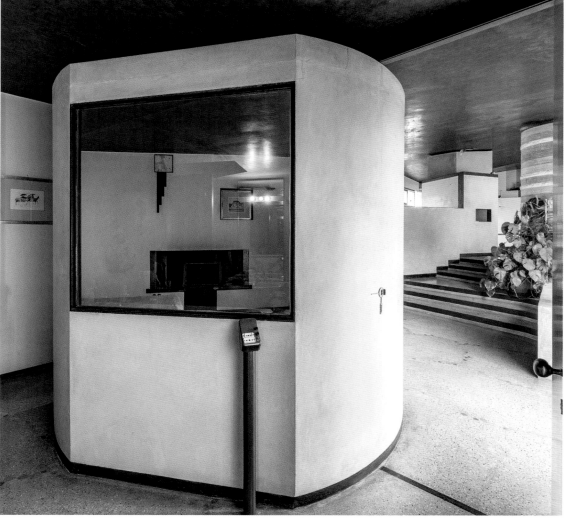

PALAZZO CHIARAMONTE (STERI)

Palermo, Sicily, 1977–88

WITH ROBERTO CALANDRA

Towards the end of his life, Scarpa worked on the restoration of the Palazzo Chiaramonte, a palace originally built in the fourteenth century. Also known as the Steri, from the Sicilian term *hosterium*, meaning a fortified palace, the historic building was notably used as the headquarters and prison of the Inquisition in the seventeenth and eighteenth centuries. In the mid-1970s, a group of architects including Roberto Calandra (1915–2015) began the renovation for the University of Palermo, and they invited Scarpa to contribute.

His contribution is most clearly seen in the entrance hall. He designed this space and its gate using an articulated sequence of stairs and landings to overcome the difference in height between the street and the internal courtyard. He thus introduced a complexity to the spatial exploration of the historic building, designing a multi-level lobby inside the large portal above the entrance, which also articulates this space vertically. Scarpa also designed the gratings that divide the internal spaces and for the Gothic external openings.

ENTRANCE TO THE FACULTY OF LITERATURE AND PHILOSOPHY, CA' FOSCARI UNIVERSITY

Venice, Italy, 1976–78

COMPLETED BY GUIDO PIETROPOLI

Scarpa drew attention to the entrance of the Faculty of Literature and Philosophy at Ca' Foscari University by creating an adjacent wall in white marble, pierced with round holes to allow light to enter the interior hall. The door itself is framed by typically Scarpian geometric mouldings, which create a point of focus among the diverse architectures of the site, which include the adjacent sixteenth-century Church of San Sebastiano, a bridge over the canal and the three-storey faculty building. This was one of Scarpa's last designs and was completed by Guido Pietropoli after his death.

ENTRANCE TO THE ISTITUTO UNIVERSITARIO DI ARCHITETTURA DI VENEZIA (IUAV)

Venice, Italy, 1976–78

With its intricate gate made from a steel-framed glass sheet and stone slab on a sliding mechanism, as well as its dramatically slanting concrete canopy, this design is an unusual play of geometries and joints. Characteristically Scarpian graduated mouldings, terminating in marble benches, feature on either side. Just beyond the entrance is a travertine path through a garden, where Scarpa made enigmatic and unexpected use of a Roman gateway that had been found during restoration of the site, which comprises a former convent and church. Scarpa laid the stone gateway down on the ground, set into a pool of water. At a time when postmodern architects were experimenting with historical architectural references, Scarpa's use of an actual historical feature functioned as a quiet criticism of arbitrary uses of such motifs.

CARLO SCARPA | THE COMPLETE BUILDINGS

ENTRANCE TO THE ISTITUTO UNIVERSITARIO DI ARCHITETTURA DI VENEZIA (IUAV)

GALLI TOMB

Genoa, Italy, 1976–78

COMPLETED BY MATTIA PASTORINO

This monolithic cube in bush-hammered Botticino marble is the tomb that Scarpa designed for the Galli family after the death of their son. The T-shaped opening in the front functions as the burial chamber and is then closed by a dark granite slab. Indeed, the tomb was designed so that the Gallis could also be entombed here upon their deaths. The arrangement of the three coffins in the T-shaped section, definitively sealed with black granite, was a symbolic design alluding to the reunion of the family in death. Mattia Pastorino, already appointed by Scarpa as the executive architect, completed the tomb after Scarpa's death.

BANCA POPOLARE DI GEMONA

Gemona del Friuli, Udine, Italy, 1978

COMPLETED BY LUCIANO GEMIN

In 1978, the year of his death, Scarpa was commissioned to rebuild the headquarters of the Banca Popolare di Gemona following the devastating Friuli earthquake of 1976. Scarpa worked on the design of the layout of the building's two structures, one of which would be used as offices and the other as a museum space. The two buildings have different characters and materials, one a square volume with a traditional touch and the other featuring large skylights that project vertically from the facade and stand out in the urban scene. The building was completed after Scarpa's death by Luciano Gemin (1928–2023).

ALTAR AND FLOOR, CHURCH OF MADONNA ADDOLORATA AL TORRESINO

Padua, Italy, 1978

Scarpa designed a new altar and floor for the early eighteenth-century church of Madonna Addolorata al Torresino in Padua. The flooring, composed of polychrome marble, rearticulates a design principle also used by Scarpa at the Fondazione Querini Stampalia, where the overall outline of the mosaic mirrors the shape of the building's central plan. The altar, standing within eight Corinthian columns beneath a cupola, is a table-like structure with double steel and brass legs supporting a black marble top covered with a glass plate.

MATERIALITY AND MEMORIES

Carlo Capovilla in Conversation with Emiliano Bugatti
Venice, 27 October 2021

The Augusto Capovilla carpentry workshop in Venice, who worked with Carlo Scarpa from the 1930s to the 1970s, is where most of the wooden elements of the architect's work were produced. It is located a short distance from Scarpa's former home on Rio Marin, in the *sestiere* (district) of Santa Croce in the city's historic centre. Owing to this proximity, Scarpa would visit the workshop daily to discuss, draw and realise the parts required for his projects. Today, Augusto Capovilla is led by Carlo Capovilla, an architect and the fourth generation of craftsmen-owners at the workshop. He has been involved in the restoration of several of Scarpa's works, the most notable perhaps being the Brion Tomb in San Vito di Altivole, Treviso.

Emiliano Bugatti: What relationship did you have with Carlo Scarpa?

Carlo Capovilla: I never knew Scarpa personally, so what I carry over are things that were told to me by my father and grandfather, Gianni and Carlo Capovilla, who worked with him directly.

EB: How did your firm work with Scarpa, and what kind of collaboration did he have with the carpenters there?

CC: Scarpa used to come to the workshop himself, and he was definitely very interested in the relationship with the carpenters. The mediation of my father, who was an architect like me, played an important role. He didn't interfere with Scarpa's decisions, but it made it easier that some of the carpenters could say, with fewer scruples, 'This cannot be done!' This phrase would certainly create debate in the shop, and Scarpa would probably respond with something like: 'But we can do it here for the first time!' Working on the restoration of several Scarpa works, I was able to see with my own eyes many of the technical solutions that had been conceived. This was an extremely interesting experience for me personally because it allowed me to hold in my hands the original pieces that had been produced decades earlier and try to understand what the original technical problems had been, the characteristics of the different woods, and guess or deduce what instructions Scarpa had given the carpenter. During restoration, we also discovered details that had originally been designed differently by Scarpa: we could identify parts that had been drawn differently and later changed in the making of the pieces, and we could see why this had been done. But there were also the occasional details where we couldn't understand how the craftsperson had agreed to do them, that were clearly problematic in that sense.

EB: Can you tell me which works you were involved in restoring?

CC: I don't remember the precise chronology, but we restored the Venice Biennale ticket office, the Fondazione Querini Stampalia, the Olivetti shop, the Brion Tomb, the Balboni house – and other works, all in Venice. For some structures, it was a simple matter of maintenance work; for others, it was necessary to replace entire parts that

OPPOSITE. View of the Augusto Capovilla workshop from the glass door of the office.

had deteriorated. Though among the most demanding projects, the Brion Tomb was an amazing experience.

ABOVE. Carlo Capovilla shows some gratings.

OPPOSITE. Inside the Augusto Capovilla workshop.

EB: The replacement of the wooden pyramidal roof inside the chapel (pp. 270–71, 332) was, I imagine, an exciting task. Could you tell us about it?

CC: Yes. The wooden roof was undoubtedly one instance where we hadn't figured out how it was assembled until we disassembled it. First of all, the perimeter of the wooden structure's base is larger than the perimeter of the concrete structure directly beneath it, and moreover there was not a single screw visible. When we started the restoration, the wooden roof, 'fortunately', was rotten at the top because of an infiltration of water. We entered inside with a micro camera, and we could see some stirrups. At the top of the pyramid, a square about 50 by 50 centimetres (20 by 20 in.), is a skylight. We found some screws there, and we hypothesised that the wooden part was actually hanging from the roof. Actually, after a lot of investigation, we realised that the whole wooden structure was made up of four parts that could be dismantled. We discovered this because a piece of wood a few dozen centimetres from the base of the pyramid was different – in fact it was screwed in with hidden screws. Once freed from the upper piece, the structure could be disassembled section by section. It was difficult work, because there were no executive drawings. Some surveys had been done over the years, but those drawings don't tell you how the structure was built.

EB: In my opinion, when it's not clear how some parts are assembled in Scarpa's work, it creates a sort of magical aura. The beauty of the unexpected is fundamental to the architectural aesthetic; it's one of the most important aspects for distinguishing ordinary from extraordinary objects.

CC: There are many other details that were difficult to understand. It was only through the work of restoration that we could enter into the true logic of the construction.

EB: One of the notable aspects of Scarpa's work is the presence of what we might call the wisdom of the workshop, as in the Gothic world. In his modernity there's something archaic that contributes to the richness of his architecture.

CC: This old-fashioned or antiquated aspect was characteristic of Scarpa's work. He was a witness to another world – not only the world of craftsmanship but a world where the role of the architect was different, too.

EB: Yes – whereas today, architectural offices draw buildings, but certain details are crafted or fabricated by someone else, who knows where in the world, and the piece arrives directly on site for assembly. Changing topic, what did you discover about the woods Scarpa used?

CC: We found all kinds of woods. He used fir, of course, but in some cases he used ebony or pearwood, like in the Brion Tomb. For instance, the wooden pyramid we previously discussed is in pear and ebony. For the windows of the chapel he used teak, while the pavilion on the water is made of larch with plywood panels (pp. 274–75). He also used teak in the Olivetti Showroom. We found that Scarpa mainly used larch for the exterior parts of his Venetian works. The wooden elements of the Venezuela Pavilion, for example, are made of larch. He also used teak when there was a possibility that the parts might get wet from rising water, as we know can happen in this city.

EB: Are there any pieces here in the workshop that were made according to Scarpa's design but which then became part of your own output?

CC: We have here a Scarpa chair prototype, but the design wasn't improved on and it was never produced. There are also some gratings: for instance, at the Olivetti Showroom there was a grating made by the Anfodillo [carpentry] workshop [in Cannaregio; now closed]. We restored it and subsequently used it as a model for other pieces for our own production. The grating, which naturally has its origins in shipbuilding here in Venice, as I imagine is also the case in other cities, was interpreted by Scarpa by progressively increasing the complexity of the wood joint. We restored a beautiful example for his Gallerie dell'Accademia, but it was later removed. But yes, in Venice there's a tradition of making gratings, and Scarpa designed new interpretations of this architectural element that was used as a screen. At that time the cost of work was different, and there was also the willingness to spend afternoons chatting in the laboratory in order to improve a piece or a prototype. There were artisans willing to listen to him and to embark on a path of professional growth with his projects.

Paolo Zanon and Francesco Zanon in Conversation with Emiliano Bugatti
Venice, 27 October 2021

Officina Zanon Gino is a blacksmith's workshop owned by Paolo and Francesco Zanon in Cannaregio, the most northerly of the six *sestieri* in Venice's historic centre. Paolo and Francesco, now both in their eighties, had the honour of working with Carlo Scarpa for more than two decades and as such are able to give direct testimony of how he worked. They produced many of the most impressive metal details designed by the Italian architect. They learned from Scarpa, but at the same time they suggested solutions to the problems he presented to them. It was a mutual dialogue, the outcome of which was some of the most outstanding architectural detailing of the period. The Zanon brothers are still active in their workshop at the time of writing. Visiting them with Luigi Guzzardi, we found them full of energy and anecdotes about their special working relationship with Scarpa; as such, the most interesting aspects of the discussion were those that emerged freely from their stories and memories.

Emiliano Bugatti: To start our conversation, did Carlo Scarpa come here to the workshop with working drawings or sketches?

Paolo Zanon: He rarely came to the workshop – it was more common for me to run after him, even in other cities!

EB: What role did you play in the design process of Scarpa's metalwork pieces?

PZ: When he showed us a drawing of what he wanted to do, we often realised by discussing the project that to produce the object would be very expensive. So we tried together to lower the costs, and when we got to a point that was satisfactory for both of us, that was the moment to begin work. To tell you the truth, he brought only a few drawings; a simple sketch was enough for us. There were many times when he had to go to the station from IUAV university, naturally on foot, and we followed him while he drew sketches to tell us how to proceed with the work! I remember once it was the support, a kind of column, for the *Amore-Attis* statue by Donatello, a sculpture by the Renaissance master that was to be displayed in the Italian Pavilion during Expo 67 in Montreal.

EB: Are there any works you did with Scarpa that you continued to produce beyond your collaboration with the architect?

Francesco Zanon: We reproduced several parts that we had originally made for Scarpa. Some of these were for restorations. For example, we redid the graphic logo that you find on the sliding gate of the entrance to the Brion Tomb complex – near the chapel where the family members' coffins enter for burial – but then it ended up remaining in the workshop because we were actually able to repair the original. I also reproduced certain pieces that I particularly liked, because every metal object designed by 'the Professor', as we used to call Scarpa, is like a work of art – if you take the individual piece out of the overall composition, it becomes an artwork to display, whether at home or in an exhibition. Sometimes, I show pieces we did in the past to architects who visit our shop. I ask if they can guess the function, and because of the complexity of the pieces, they're often unable to identify even a simple doorstop!

EB: We also interviewed Carlo Capovilla, who said that some of the wooden gratings Scarpa designed ended up becoming part of the workshop's standard production. Do you have anything similar here at Officina Zanon?

FZ: We fabricated the metal grating at the main entrance to the Olivetti Showroom (p. 152), and we later realised other similar gratings, but not with the same measurements and proportions as the Professor's design. That one is perfect. Everything we realised for him was so special that we didn't use it later for other works.
    When I met Scarpa, I was fourteen, and at that time many architects would come to the workshop, but later I understood how different he was from the others. There were times when we'd work into the night to realise pieces for his exhibition projects. We'd produce all the pieces for the display of artworks, mainly metal supports, in three or

PREVIOUS, LEFT. View from below of the wooden pyramidal roof of the Brion Tomb chapel, San Vito d'Altivole, Treviso.

PREVIOUS, RIGHT. Detail of the sliding panel at the entrance to the Istituto Universitario di Architettura di Venezia (IUAV), Venice.

OPPOSITE, TOP. Interior of the Officina Zanon Gino workshop.

OPPPOSITE, BOTTOM. An old lathe at the Zanon workshop.

so weeks before an opening, and we'd be working for entire days, including through the night! He used to come to the workshop with the measurements of a particular artwork; then we'd go to the museum or gallery – the Museo Correr, for example – and, with Scarpa's sketches of the supports, we'd decide on the measurements and then go back to make the pieces. Scarpa was a total architect. He understood every type of material, he could converse with everyone involved on a construction site. He used some silicon brass sheeting for the Olivetti Showroom. This is a material used in the Venetian Arsenal, but we hadn't come across it!

EB: It was a golden age for architecture, not only because of Scarpa's vast knowledge but also because of collaborations such as yours.

FZ: We were lucky, but he was too because he found workers like us. But before us, our father was a great craftsman. Imagine: to create the metalwork for the Olivetti Showroom, he had to build machines to do the required work. He built tools specifically to make certain special joints. Sixty years ago, there were no commercial milling machines available. Although ours was a fairly well-equipped workshop, we were a bit lacking as far as tools – there were three lathes, a milling machine and an automatic hacksaw made by our father. It took great effort, creativity and ingenuity to produce things that today can be easily made with a milling machine. Our father wasn't an alchemist, but he knew how to design new machines, and he understood the Professor very well, supporting him and managing to achieve what he wanted. I remember, the lathes worked with only one motor; there was only one drive belt, and by pulling the levers, one lathe was activated and the other was blocked. The engines were rare in those times, and once the belts were worn out, they were repurposed as the soles of shoes. This is history!

PZ: I worked with Scarpa for 25 years.

FZ: For me, the period since Scarpa has been a diminished one. Today, there aren't jobs like that – ones that give me the same satisfaction.

EB: When you were restoring works that you had originally made many years earlier, did you have to make changes? Did you improve upon the design of certain pieces, to avoid future maintenance problems or other issues that had developed with use?

CARLO SCARPA | THE COMPLETE BUILDINGS

TOP. Paolo, left, and
Francesco Zanon, right,
explaining how to assemble,
without screws, a piece
Scarpa designed for the
mezzanine gallery of the
Olivetti Showroom in Venice.

BOTTOM. Interior of the
Zanon workshop.

PZ: One example was in the Brion Tomb: in the openings with the mosaics (p. 267), the internal structure of the concrete was made of iron bars, but with water ingress they expand and there's a risk of the concrete being damaged. So we removed the iron parts and used stainless steel. The brass parts held up well, however; we changed a few pieces, but the final result is exactly as it was before the interventions.

EB: What do you feel when you rediscover these works from fifty years ago?

PZ: It was just normal – the daily routine of work!

FZ: Time worries me, unfortunately. I think: the pyramids have been there for 4,000 years, but works like those of Carlo Scarpa must be maintained correctly and constantly. For fifty years since the Professor died, interventions have had to be made at the Brion Tomb – if this hadn't been done, half the cemetery would have been lost! The Brions' son,

Ennio, who is still alive, has undertaken the very demanding task of restoring the entire complex, and he has spent a lot of money to try and prevent further degradation. But what will happen when there are no members of the family left?

EB: Is ruin perhaps the fate of this architecture?

PZ: I'm sure it will be owned by FAI, the Italian Environmental Fund, as is the case with the Olivetti Showroom. I hope it will be preserved in the future.

FZ: I went to visit the Olivetti Showroom with some architects. They were talking about the windows. I asked if they had seen the corner of the shop window, and we went outside and I showed them the interlocking profiles. Architects, it's the Professor! He is in the details. You wouldn't believe the contraptions underneath the shelves that hold the typewriters – you'd need a mirror on the ground to appreciate them!

PZ: (*Walking around the workshop, Francesco and Paolo point out particular objects that were made for Scarpa*) This is a piece from the Olivetti Showroom. It's the structure that supports the upper gallery (p. 337 top, and below). There's not a single screw; it's made of different interlocking pieces of iron and brass. We did this because some pieces are conical, and therefore if they had been fitted together with screws the whole composition would not have flowed as it does.

FZ: Towards the end of the monumental project of constructing the tomb, Mrs Brion was getting a little tired of the various delays. But after Scarpa's death, she said to me, 'What melancholy. I'd like to do it all over again!' Despite the difficulties and vicissitudes of such a complicated job, she would have done it all again, just to keep the contact with the architect alive.

It's curious that the first funeral celebrated in the Brion complex was that of Scarpa himself. It was like signing his most important work. That's where you can find his modest tomb – in an inconspicuous corner of the complex.

BELOW. Paolo Zanon's hand with part of the structure designed for the gallery of the Olivetti Showroom.

OPPOSITE. Detail of the mahogany-finished door in the Aula Manlio Capitolo, Venice Courthouse. The opening mechanism represents a sword and scales.

CHRONOLOGY

Buildings marked with an asterisk are not currently accessible owing to restoration works or for reasons of structural integrity.

WORKS

| Sfriso shop,*
Venice,
1932 | Casa Pelizzari,
Venice,
1942 | Casa Bellotto,
Venice,
1944–46 | Banca Cattolica
del Veneto,
Tarvisio,
1947–49 |

ESSENTIAL BIOGRAPHY

	1932	1933–34	1948
Carlo Scarpa is born in Venice on 2 June 1906 to Emma Novello and Antonio Scarpa. He spends much of his childhood in Vicenza, returning to Venice after his mother's death in 1919. In 1926 he graduates from the Accademia di Belle Arti di Venezia with a diploma in architectural drawing. He begins his career as an assistant to Guido Cirilli (1871–1954), his former teacher, in the new Scuola Superiore di Architettura.	Becomes artistic director of Venini & C., a company producing traditional Murano glass. Between 1932 and 1947 he designs numerous decorative and functional glass objects for the firm and pioneers new techniques and styles, many of which would go on to be exhibited at the Triennale di Milano and the Venice Biennale.	Becomes a professor of drawing and interior decoration at the Scuola Superiore di Architettura, which in 1940 becomes the Istituto Universitario di Architettura (IUAV). In 1934 he marries Onorina 'Nini' Lazzari, and the following year their son, Tobia, is born; he will later become a noted designer and architect.	In 1948 Scarpa designs an exhibition of works by Paul Klee, displayed in the Central Pavilion in the Giardini for the 24th Venice Biennale. It is the start of a long collaboration with the biennale that lasts until 1972.

| 1906 | 1930S | | 1940S | |

| 1922–43 Italy governed by the Fascist regime of Benito Mussolini | 1939–45 Second World War | 1948 Constitution of the Italian Repub |

MODERN MASTERS IN VENICE: FRANK LLOYD WRIGHT, LE CORBUSIER & LOUIS KAHN

1940S

In the 1940s Scarpa explores the work of Frank Lloyd Wright, discovering him thanks to Bruno Zevi, who has brought materials back to Italy from the USA.

| Aula Mario Baratto,
Ca' Foscari University of
Venice, 1935–37; 1955–56 | Capovilla Tomb,
Venice,
1943–44 | Gallerie
dell'Accademia,
Venice,
1945–59 | Casa Giacomuzzi,
Udine, 1947–50 |

Veritti Tomb,
Udine,
1952

Casa Ambrosini,
Venice,
1952–53

Museo Correr,
Venice,
1952–53; 1957–60

Galleria Regionale
della Sicilia, Palazzo
Abatellis, Palermo,
1953–54

Gabinetto dei
Disegni e Delle
Stampe, Uffizi
Gallery, Florence,
1956–60

1950

Prior to designing the
new ticket office for
the Venice Biennale
and interventions to its
existing Central Pavilion,
including the creation
of its Sculpture Garden
(1951–52), Scarpa designs
an Art Book Pavilion at
the Giardini in 1950; it is
destroyed by fire in 1984.

1952

Designs the installation
of the exhibition
*Antonello da Messina
e la pittura del '400* in
Sicilia at the Palazzo
Communale in Messina,
Sicily. The success of the
exhibition leads Scarpa
to win a commission
to renovate the Palazzo
Abatellis in Palermo
for use as a museum.

1950S

1948 The Marshall Plan is enacted

1950–51

After a three-month
residency at the
American Academy in
Rome in 1950, American
architect Louis Kahn
travels to Venice,
where he produces
an important series of
analytical sketches of
the Piazza San Marco.

1951

Frank Lloyd Wright is in
Italy for an exhibition of
his work at the Palazzo
Strozzi in Florence,
where he meets Scarpa.
In Venice he receives
an honorary degree
from IUAV.

1952

Angelo Masieri, a former
student and subsequent
collaborator of Scarpa's,
dies in the USA on the
way to a meeting with
Wright, whom he wants
to commission to design
his house in Venice.

In 1953, Wright, at the
invitation of Masieri's
family, designs the
Masieri Memorial in
the same building on
the Grand Canal. The
proposal is rejected by
the municipality in 1955.

Villa Bortolotto,
Udine,
1950–52

Venice Biennale
Sculpture Garden
and Ticket Office,
Venice, 1951–52
and 1952

Garden,* Casa
Guarnieri, Lido,
Venice,
1952

Casa Romanelli,
Udine,
1952–55

Venezuela
Pavilion,
Venice,
1954–56

Council Chamber,
Palazzo della
Provincia di Parma,
1955–56

Canova Plaster
Cast Gallery,
Possagno,
1955–57

Church of San
Giovanni Battista,
Firenzuola,
1955–66

Olivetti
Showroom,
Venice,
1957–58

Museo di
Castelvecchio,
Verona, 1958–64;
1967–69; 1973–75

1956

Owing to the fact
that he never sat his
architectural licence
exams, Scarpa is
denounced by the
Chamber of Architects
of the Veneto region for
practising the profession
without a licence. In the
same year, he is awarded
the Olivetti Prize for
Architecture.

1957

In 1957, Adriano Olivetti,
owner of the company
and a philanthropist,
commissions Scarpa
to design a shop and
showroom for the
display of the firm's
typewriter products.

1958

Designs an exhibition
in the Reggia wing
of the Museo del
Castelvecchio in Verona.
Thanks to the support
of the museum's
director, Licisco
Magagnato, Scarpa is
also commissioned to
restore and reorganise
the entire complex, a
long project realised in
three phases.

1950S

1953 Italy joins the European common market for coal and steel

1958–63 Italian economic miracl

1959

Le Corbusier is invited
to design a new hospital
for the city of Venice.

Base for the
Sculpture
of the Partisan
Woman
(Leoncillo
Leonardi),
Venice,
1955

Aula Manlio
Capitolo,
Courthouse,
Venice,
1955–57

Villa Veritti,
Udine,
1955–61

Church of Nostra
Signora del
Cadore, Belluno,
1956–61

Camping Fusina,
Venice,
1957–59

Courtyard, Grand
Hotel Minerva,
Florence,
1958–61

Zilio Tomb,
Udine,
1960

Gavina Showroom,
Bologna,
1961–63

Gallo House
and Studio,*
Vicenza,
1962–65

Museo Revoltella,
Trieste,
1963–78

Zentner House,
Zurich,
1964–68

1960

1961

1962

1964

Designs the exhibition of Frank Lloyd Wright at the XII Triennale de Milano. In the same year, Scarpa designs an exhibition of the German architect Erich Mendelsohn for the 30th Venice Biennale.

Scarpa has been designing both custom furniture and objects for mass production since the earliest days of his career. In 1960

he becomes honorary president of the furniture company Gavina, and from 1968 to 1977 he will design furniture for both Gavina and Simon International (established by Dino Gavina).

Curates the exhibition *Il senso del colore, il governo delle acque* (The Sense of Colour, The Governance of Water) for the Veneto Pavilion at Expo 61 (also known as Italia 61 for its celebration of the centenary of Italian unification). As part of the display, he designs a chandelier made up of modular and sectional elements in glass, which is produced by Venini.

Awarded the IN/ARCH prize for architecture for his Galleria Regionale della Sicilia at the Palazzo Abatellis in Palermo.

Becomes Professor of Architectural Composition at IUAV, a post he will hold until 1976.

1960s

1964

Le Corbusier presents his project for the new hospital in Venice, which he has conceived as a horizontal structure raised on his signature concrete pilotis, with parts extending over the Venetian Lagoon.

Rinaldo-Lazzari Tomb,
Quero, Belluno,
1960

Fondazione
Querini Stampalia,
Venice,
1961–63

Casa Scatturin,
Venice,
1962–63

Casa Scarpa,*
Venice, 1963

Facade and tasting room,
Fondazione Edmund Mach,
San Michele all'Adige,
Trentino, 1964–66

Annex to the Casa De Benedetti-Bonaiuto, Rome, 1965–72	Offices of La Nuova Italia, Florence, 1968–72	Brion Tomb, San Vito d'Altivole, Treviso, 1969–78	Luigi Marzoli Weapons Museum, Brescia, 1971–78	Commemorative Stele, Piazza della Loggia, Brescia, 1974–77
1963	**1966**	**1967**	**1968–71**	
Among a number of unrealised projects by Scarpa is a project to renovate the Carlo Felice Theatre in Genoa, destroyed during the Second World War, which engages the architect for ten years, from 1963 to 1976. The new theatre will eventually be realised by Aldo Rossi, Ignazio Gardella and Fabio Reinhart in 1984–91.	An exhibition of Scarpa's work is shown at the Museum of Modern Art, New York.	Designs the Italian Pavilion, entitled 'La Poesia' (Poetry), at Expo 67 in Montreal. Travels to the United States, where he visits the works of Wright and meets Kahn, whom he sees again in Venice the following year. Cesare Cassina, owner of the Cassina furniture company, invites Scarpa to visit Japan for the first time in 1969.	Participates in the 34th Venice Biennale in 1968 with an exhibition of his own work. The same year, Giuseppe Brion, owner of the Brionvega electronics company, dies; his widow, Onorina Tomasin-Brion, commissions Scarpa to design a funerary complex in San Vito d'Altivole. Scarpa is awarded the honour of Royal Designer for Industry by the Royal Society of Arts, London.	In 1969, Scarpa journeys to Japan, where he meets Aldo Businaro, for whom he will later carry out the Villa Il Palazzetto project in Monselice. In 1971, becomes director of the Faculty of Architecture at IUAV, a position he will hold until 1974.

1960S   1970S

1969–70 Hot Autumn, a period of large-scale worker strikes and social unrest

1974 Piazza della Loggia, Brescia, bombed by a neo-fascist group

1968, 1972

Louis Kahn and Scarpa collaborate during the 1968 and 1972 Venice Biennales. Kahn is also commissioned to design a new Palazzo dei Congressi in Venice, completed in 1972.

Casa Balboni, Venice, 1964–74	Base for the Monument to the Partisan Woman, Venice, 1968	Masieri Memorial, Venice, 1968–78	Additions to the Villa Il Palazzetto, Monselice, Padua, 1971–78	Banca Popolare di Verona, 1973–78	Apartment Building, Vicenza, 1974–78

Staircase,*
Casa Muraro,
Venice,
1975

Palazzo
Chiaramonte
(Steri), Palermo,
1977

Entrance to
the Istituto
Universitario di
Architettura di
Venezia (IUAV),
Venice, 1966;
1976–78

Banca Popolare
di Gemona,
Gemona del Friuli,
Udine,
1978

1972–74	1977		1978
In 1972 Scarpa moves to Vicenza. In 1974 he designs the exhibition *Venezia e Bisanzio* (Venice and Byzantium) at the Palazzo Ducale, Venice. The same year, he has a solo exhibition of his works, entitled *Carlo Scarpa: architetto poeta* (Carlo Scarpa: Architect Poet), in Vicenza, London and Paris.	An exhibition of Scarpa's work is held at the Institut de l'Environnement in Paris.		An exhibition of Scarpa's work is held in Madrid. On 28 November 1978, Carlo Scarpa dies in Sendai, Japan, after accidentally falling down a flight of stairs. He is 72. According to his wishes, he is buried at San Vito d'Altivole, between the old cemetery and the Brion Tomb complex he designed. After his death, Scarpa is awarded an honorary degree in architecture from IUAV, given to the family in 1983.

1978

1978 Former prime minister Aldo Moro is kidnapped and murdered by the far-left Red Brigades

1974

Louis Kahn dedicates
a poem to Scarpa, in
which he writes: 'the
inner realization of
"Form" / The sense
of the wholeness of
inseparable elements ...
In the elements the joint
inspires ornament, its
celebration. / The detail
is in the adoration of
Nature.'

Villa Ottolenghi,
Bardolino,
1974–78

Entrance to the
Faculty of Literature
and Philosophy,
Ca' Foscari University,
Venice, 1976–78

Galli Tomb,
Genoa,
1976–78

Altar and floor, Church
of Madonna Addolorata
al Torresino, Padua, 1978

SELECT BIBLIOGRAPHY

Albertini, Bianca, and Sandro Bagnoli, *Scarpa: i musei e le esposizioni* (Milan: Jaca Book, 1992)

Bagnoli, Sandro, and Alba Di Lieto, eds, *Carlo Scarpa, Sandro Bagnoli: Il design per Dino Gavina / Design for Dino Gavina* (Venice: Silvana Editoriale, and Milan: Cinisello Balsamo, 2014)

Beltramini, Guido, and Italo Zannier, eds, *Carlo Scarpa: Architecture Atlas* (Venice: Marsilio Editori, 2006)

Carlo Scarpa, special issue of *A+U: Architecture and Urbanism* [Tokyo] (October 1985)

Carmel-Arthur, Judith, and Stefan Buzas, *Carlo Scarpa: Museo Canoviano, Possagno* (Stuttgart and London: Edition Axel Menges, 2002)

Dal Co, Francesco, and Giuseppe Mazzariol, *Carlo Scarpa: The Complete Works* (New York: Rizzoli, 1984)

Duboÿ, Philippe, ed., *Carlo Scarpa: L'art d'exposer* (Zurich: JRP Ringier, and Paris: L'Association des Amis de la Maison Rouge, 2014)

Esposito, Anselmo, and Luciano Pollifrone, 'Itinerario Domus 19: Scarpa e Venezia', *Domus* 678 (December 1986), pp. ix–xii

Filler, Martin, *Makers of Modern Architecture*, vol. II: *From Le Corbusier to Rem Koolhaas* (New York: New York Review Books, 2013)

Frampton, Kenneth, *Modern Architecture: A Critical History* (London: Thames & Hudson, 1980)

Frampton, Kenneth, *Studies in Tectonic Culture: The Poetics of Construction in Nineteenth and Twentieth Century Architecture* (Cambridge, MA: MIT Press, 1995)

Giunta, Santo, *Carlo Scarpa: A (curious) shaft of light, a golden Gonfalon, the hands and a face of a woman: Reflections on the design process and layout of Palazzo Abatellis, 1953–1954* (Venice: Marsilio, 2020)

Guzzardi, Luigi, ed., *Carlo Scarpa: tre progetti veneziani, 1942–1951* (Venice: Caffè Florian, 1996)

Köksal, Aykut, et al., *Carlo Scarpa*, Çağdaş Dünya Mimarları Dizisi [Contemporary World Architects Series] (Istanbul: Boyut Yayın Grubu, 2001)

Los, Sergio, *Carlo Scarpa* (Cologne: Taschen, 1994)

Los, Sergio, *Carlo Scarpa: guida all'architettura* (Venice: Arsenale Editrice, 1995)

Marcianò, Ada Francesca, ed., *Carlo Scarpa* (Bologna: Zanichelli, 1984)

Murphy, Richard, *Carlo Scarpa and Castelvecchio Revisited* (Edinburgh: Breakfast Mission Publishing, 2017)

Noever, Peter, ed., *Carlo Scarpa: Das Handwerk der Architektur / The Craft of Architecture*, exh. cat., MAK, Vienna (Ostfildern: Hatje Cantz, 2003)

Olsberg, Nicholas, ed., *Carlo Scarpa, Architect: Intervening with History* (Montreal: Canadian Centre for Architecture, and New York: Monacelli Press, 1999)

Pietropoli, Guido, Carla Sonego and Luigi Latini, eds, *Memoriae causa: Carlo Scarpa e il complesso monumentale Brion, 1969–1978* (Treviso: Fondazione Benetton, 2007)

Saito, Yutaka, *Carlo Scarpa* (Amsterdam: Idea Books, 1997)

Scarpa, Carlo, *Frammenti 1926/1978*, ed. Arrigo Rudi and Francesca Fenaroli, special issue of *Rassegna*, year III, no. 7 (July 1981)

Tafuri, Manfredo, *History of Italian Architecture, 1944–1985* (Cambridge, MA: MIT Press, 1989)

Schultz, Anne Catrin, *Carlo Scarpa: Layers* (Stuttgart: Edition Axel Menges, 2010)

ACKNOWLEDGEMENTS

First of all, we would like to thank Luigi Guzzardi for his fundamental support in this long journey from 2018 to 2023; like Virgil for Dante, he was an important guide in our exploration of the complex world of Carlo Scarpa. A special thank you also goes to Davide Arra for his kindness and willingness to take Cemal Emden around northern Italy.

We wish to thank all the private owners and public institutions who opened their doors to Emden and granted him permission to photograph the spaces. In particular, for their efforts in mediating with owners and institutions, we thank Federico Businaro, Alba Di Lieto, Guido Pietropoli, Edoardo Zentner and once again Luigi Guzzardi.

We express our gratitude to the Istituto Italiano di Cultura di Istanbul, and in particular its director, Salvatore Schirmo, for supporting the event 'Scarpa Diyaloglari' (Dialogues on Scarpa), held in Istanbul in October 2022 and organised by the IstanbulSMD (Istanbul Association of Architects in Private Practice).

Last but not least, thank you to Prestel Publishing for believing in this project from the early stages, in particular Andrew Hansen and, later in the process, Rochelle Roberts and Aimee Selby, for their work on our texts, and Peter Dawson, who designed the book you now hold in your hands.

ABOUT THE AUTHORS

Emiliano Bugatti is an architect and was an academic in Turkey between 2008 and 2018. He has written about the architecture and urbanism of the eastern and southern Mediterranean Basin from the early modern period to the modernisation of the nineteenth and twentieth centuries. In 2010, with the TEGET architecture firm in Istanbul, he won the competition to design the Izmir Opera House; the building is under construction. He currently teaches art history and drawing in Ravenna, Italy.

Cemal Emden is an architect who specialises in photographing architecture, interior design, landscape and furniture. His photography has been widely published in magazines, books and exhibitions both in his home country of Turkey and internationally. His previous books include *Le Corbusier: The Complete Buildings* (2017) and *The Essential Louis Kahn* (2021), both published by Prestel.

Jale N. Erzen is a painter and art historian. She was formerly president of the International Association for Aesthetics and editor of the Turkish art journal *Boyut*. She is a recipient of the French Ministry of Culture's Order of Arts and Letters and has written on architecture for Turkish and international publications, including the book *Sinan, Ottoman Architect: An Aesthetic Analysis* (2004).

INDEX

© 2024 Prestel Verlag, Munich · London · New York,
A member of Penguin Random House Verlagsgruppe GmbH
Neumarkter Strasse 28 · 81673 Munich

© for the text by Emiliano Bugatti and Jale N. Erzen, 2024
© for artwork by Cemal Emden, 2024

Front cover: Interior of Gavina Shop, Bologna
Back cover: Brion Tomb, San Vito d'Altivole, Treviso
Page 2: Chapel exterior, Brion Tomb, San Vito d'Altivole, Treviso

A CIP catalogue record for this book is available from the British Library.

Editorial direction: Rochelle Roberts
Copyediting: Aimee Selby
Design: Peter Dawson, with Ronja Ronning, www.gradedesign.com
Production: Luisa Klose
Separations: Reproline Mediateam, Munich
Printing and binding: Livonia Print, Riga
Paper: Magno Matt

Penguin Random House Verlagsgruppe FSC® N001967

Printed in Latvia

ISBN 978-3-7913-7714-8

www.prestel.com